Buttercream
Petals

ACKNOWLEDGEMENTS

Thank you to my business partner and life partner, my husband Anand, for being my pillar of strength; thank you to my sister, Nathalia, who has always been at my side; and to my official cake taster, our darling son, Madhavankutty.

My heart goes out to my wonderful family – my Amma, Acha, Raj, my husband's parents, and my dearest friends for always cheering me on and your unconditional support.

I dedicate this book to my students and social media followers – I am so grateful for your overwhelming support and enthusiasm.

Thanks to Search Press, Katie and Beth, for your patience and encouragement; our awesome photographer, Mark, and designer Juan for visualizing and capturing the projects so beautifully.

Thanks to my preferred UK suppliers for providing excellent tools and materials for the projects featured in this book: Sweet Success UK (www.sweetsuccess.uk.com) for ready-to-decorate sponge and fruit cake bases and cake supplies; and to Cake Craft World (www.cakecraftworld.co.uk) – for their cake-decorating supplies.

Buttercream Petals

Vibrant flowers for stunning cakes using piping and palette-knife painting

Neetha Syam

SEARCH PRESS

First published in 2021
Search Press Limited
Wellwood, North Farm Road,
Tunbridge Wells, Kent TN2 3DR

ISBN: 978-1-78221-824-1
ebook ISBN: 978-1-78126-791-2

Suppliers

If you have difficulty in obtaining any of the materials
and equipment mentioned in this book, then please
visit the Search Press website for details of suppliers:
www.searchpress.com

Extra copies of the template on page 108 are available
from www.bookmarkedhub.com

You are invited to visit the author's website:
buttercreampetals.com

Publishers' note

All the step-by-step photographs in this book feature
the author, Neetha Syam, demonstrating how to make
buttercream petals. No models have been used.

The projects in this book have been made using metric
weights and volumes; imperial weights and volumes
have been calculated following standard conversion
practices. Where given, imperial conversions are often
rounded to the nearest ⅛oz for ease of use; however, if
you need more exact measurements, there are excellent
converters online that you can use. Always use either
metric or imperial measurements, not a combination
of both.

Contents

Introduction

I am so glad that you are reading these words, that you have decided to turn these pages and discover how to create edible buttercream art. I hope this book inspires you and motivates you.

Before we start, I would like to tell you a little about myself. My cake journey started almost a decade ago when this uncontrollable urge overtook me to bake and decorate cakes incessantly. I took any opportunity to bake for my family, friends, colleagues, extended family, friends of friends… I just couldn't ignore the call!

In 2015, soon after my maternity leave, I decided to resign from my job as a chartered accountant to make a career out of doing the two things I love the most – cake-decorating and writing. The biggest plus point of this decision was that I could spend as much time as I wanted with my cute little baby (who is not so little any more, but still very cute!).

I am entirely self-taught; whatever I share with you are my own creations and discoveries, all tried and tested. 'Buttercream Petals' was initially a social media platform where I shared my artistic buttercream experiments.

My breakthrough happened in 2017 when my cake design won Best in Category at the

Cake International show, based on its taste and design qualities. The following year, I won Best in Class in the International Salon Culinaire competition, based on the design and taste of my signature buttercream.

I was ecstatic when people from across the globe began to express interest in learning my techniques. I started running classes across the UK; then, to reach students far and wide, I launched my extensive Buttercream Petals Online School (www.buttercreampetals.com), where I teach everything from baking to buttercream art. My students range from hobby bakers to home-baking businesses and professional chefs.

Everything in this book features buttercream. I love buttercream as it lets me live up to my motto that a cake should always taste better than it looks!

It's such a versatile medium to work with, too – from flower piping to palette-knife painting, there is so much you can do with it!

I am hugely inspired by nature, whether it be the myriad flowers or foliage or the colourful birds and butterflies. I love to portray the harmonious bond between human beings and nature, too. One of my most popular and best-loved designs is a painted buttercream lady in a floral gown. I also love featuring 'a moment' from everyday happenings in nature, such as birds resting on the branch of a tree or a butterfly sneaking in to collect the nectar from a full bloom. Any of these moments can inspire a buttercream design.

May this be the beginning of many buttercream creations on your part; let's get started!

Essential Equipment

Buttercream cake decorating doesn't need a lot of expensive tools: it is more about the techniques than the tools. Below is a comprehensive list of the tools that you will need for the projects in this book.

1. Stand mixer or handheld mixer   You will need an electric handheld mixer or a stand mixer to make the buttercream.

2. Cocktail sticks (toothpicks)   These are a great tool for transferring colours as well as for correcting any buttercream mishaps. They can also be used to support a flower as it is lifted onto a cake design.

3. Piping nozzles   You can buy nozzles of any brand as long as the shape looks similar to the nozzles I use in this book (see opposite).

4. Piping bags   You can use any piping bags of your choice: disposable plastic ones or reusable silicone ones.

5. Couplers   Couplers are small tools that can be attached to a piping bag so that you can easily attach a nozzle to the bag.

6. Flower nail   Buttercream flowers can be piped onto a flower nail paired with a greaseproof paper square and frozen, before being transferred on to a cake.

7. Palette knives   There are palette knives made specially for cake decorating, which you can use when covering cakes; but for palette-knife painting, you will need artists' palette knives, which can be bought at any art store.

8. Plastic chopping board or glass tray   This is a handy tool on which to do your palette-knife painting, as it is flat and smooth.

9. Cake smoother   You can buy metal or plastic cake smoothers: I prefer plastic as it's lightweight and allows me to work more seamlessly around my cakes.

10. Bowl   You can use any bowl to mix colours with buttercream and to prepare the buttercream itself.

11. Sieve   A sieve can be used for sifting icing sugar, which is key to achieving smooth buttercream.

12. Cake turntable   This is a must for smoothing cakes. I recommend that you invest in a metal turntable, as it rotates more smoothly than a plastic one.

13. Cake drums/boards   You can use cake boards under smaller cakes, and cake drums under heavier or tiered cakes.

14. Dowels   Dowels ensure that the weight of the top tier of a cake does not cause it to fall onto the bottom tier (see page 21). You can use wooden or plastic dowels.

15. Flower lifter (or scissors)   Use this to transfer your piped flowers onto your cake.

16. Spatula   You can use a spoon for mixing the buttercream as you make it, but I find a silicone or plastic spatula is best for mixing buttercream.

17. Cake leveller   This is a great tool for ensuring that you cut even layers of cake.

18. Scissors   Small scissors are great for cutting greaseproof paper or design templates, and also for transferring piped flowers onto a cake if you do not own a flower lifter.

19. Measuring spoons   A set of tablespoons and teaspoons are ideal for buttercream making and cake baking.

20. Scales   Any food weighing scale would do the job in making sure we can measure the ingredients correctly for buttercream making and baking.

21. Cake lifter   A great tool that ensures that the delicate sponge layers don't break or get damaged as you handle the cake, either when assembling or transferring it.

22. Paintbrush   You can use any artists' paintbrush when working with buttercream – I have used a paintbrush specifically to smooth the buttercream onto the cake when painting the *Hydrangea Lady*, pages 108–113.

3

Look at the shape of the nozzle – this is the most important quality. Any brand of nozzle will do.

7

You can use artists' palette knives for painting with buttercream.

Cake Recipes

Before sharing any recipes, I would like to share with you my Top Ten baking tips. These are tips that I have gathered along the way, through trial and error, and through the wisdom shared in the many baking forums and social media groups I have been part of. This is purely about the science of cake-making: regardless of the recipe that you follow, these are some of the key elements that I recommend you always bear in mind while baking.

Neetha's Top Ten Tips for Baking Success

1. **All of the ingredients for the cake need to be at room temperature**   You may already know this, but let me tell you, all ingredients – meaning your butter, eggs, milk, buttermilk, sour cream... anything that you add to the batter – need to be at room temperature before you begin.

2. **Warm the milk slightly**   If a recipe calls for milk, warm the milk slightly in a microwave for thirty seconds or less. It should be warm, but not hot. This is the key to a moist bake.

3. **Replace butter with vegetable shortening**   If you live in a cold country, you may have noticed that cakes made with butter can go really hard after the cake cools down. I have found that using a vegetable shortening such as Stork (in the UK), Crisco (in the US) or Delicious (in India) results in a much fluffier and softer cake.

4. **Don't overbeat the batter**   Once you add the flour, you should beat the batter at medium speed for ten seconds or less. That's it. If any ingredients remain unmixed at the bottom of the bowl, fold them in with a spatula. This is very important. Overbeating the batter can alter the cake texture to make it quite rubbery and dense.

5. **Always use vanilla paste**   Many of us use vanilla essence or extract for baking: but these are alcohol-based flavourings which will evaporate considerably in the oven. Instead, use a vanilla paste, with vanilla pods in it, which will enhance the flavour of the cake.

6. **Check the temperature of the oven**   I tend to bake at 180°C/350°F/Fan 160°C/Gas mark 4, whether it be cakes or cupcakes. I have found that a higher oven temperature results in a hard crust on the cake that then needs to be trimmed off. A lower temperature results in a soft bake, so there will be no need to trim anything!

7. **Preheat the oven**   for 10 minutes before putting the cake in.

8. **Place a pan of water on the bottom rack of the oven**   This results in a moist environment and evens the temperature in the oven, resulting in a fantastic, flat bake: this is the secret to flat-top cakes and cupcakes.

9. **Do not open the oven while baking**   This comes with practice but you should follow the baking time given in the recipe and only open the oven once that time is up. You can then check if the cake is done by inserting a fork or skewer which should come out clean. Opening the oven while baking results in a sunken middle.

10. **Cool the cake on a wire rack**   Always cool the cake in the cake tins for five minutes first, and then invert them onto a wire rack. Transferring cakes or cupcakes to a flat plate or tray to cool will result in moisture (steam) building up at the base of the cake.

Sponge cake

INGREDIENTS

200g (7oz) caster sugar

230g (8⅛oz) butter

230g (8⅛oz) self-raising flour

4 large eggs

1tbsp vanilla essence

1tsp baking powder

¼tsp salt

INSTRUCTIONS

1. Preheat oven to 180°C/350°F/Fan 160°C/Gas mark 4.

2. Cream butter and sugar till light and fluffy (5 minutes).

3. Add eggs one by one, mixing well after each addition.

4. Add flour, baking powder, salt and vanilla essence – add cocoa powder if you are baking a chocolate sponge cake. Mix well, paying attention so as not to overbeat the batter.

5. Bake for about 20–23 minutes if in two 20cm (8in) sandwich tins, or until an inserted skewer comes out clean. If you are using deep cake pans, bake for about 40 minutes, or until an inserted skewer comes out clean.

Chocolate sponge cake

INGREDIENTS

200g (7oz) caster sugar

230g (8⅛oz) butter

190g (6¾oz) self-raising flour

40g (1⅜oz) cocoa powder

4 large eggs

1tbsp vanilla essence

1tsp baking powder

¼tsp salt

Vanilla cupcakes

(Makes 12 cupcakes)

INGREDIENTS

150g (5¼oz) caster sugar

150g (5¼oz) butter

150g (5¼oz) self-raising flour

2 large eggs

1tbsp vanilla essence

1tsp baking powder

60ml (2fl.oz) milk

Chocolate cupcakes

(Makes 12 cupcakes)

INGREDIENTS

150g (5¼oz) caster sugar

150g (5¼oz) butter

110g (3⅞oz) self-raising flour

2 large eggs

40g (1⅜oz) cocoa powder

1btsp vanilla essence

1tsp baking powder

60ml (2fl.oz) milk

INSTRUCTIONS

1. Preheat oven to 180°C/350°F/Fan 160°C/Gas mark 4.

2. Cream butter and sugar till light and fluffy (4 minutes).

3. Add lightly beaten eggs and vanilla extract, and mix.

4. Add flour and milk, alternately. Add cocoa powder for chocolate cupcakes. Mix well, paying attention so as not to overbeat the batter.

5. Line a cupcake tin with cupcake cases.

6. Pour in the batter, filling up to two-thirds of the cupcake cases.

7. Bake for about 23 minutes or until a skewer inserted comes out clean.

Buttercream Recipes

This is a basic buttercream recipe: simple enough to make, with the right amount of sweetness. It is a great recipe to start with and everything you see in the book is created using this recipe.

My signature buttercream recipe is a little bit more technical and is taught at my online school.

Basic buttercream recipe

INGREDIENTS

250g (8⅞oz) butter (**a**)

250g (8⅞oz) vegetable shortening (**b**)

2tbsp water – or double cream
or milk (**c**)

1tbsp vanilla extract (**d**)

500g (17⅝oz) icing sugar (**e**)

INSTRUCTIONS

1. Beat butter for a total of 3 minutes, stopping after 1 minute to scrape the sides and bottom of the bowl with a spatula. The butter should be slightly cold, not too soft: this will help the butter to whip up well.

2. Add vegetable shortening and beat for 1 minute. Again, scrape the sides and bottom of the bowl with the spatula.

3. Add water (or double cream, or milk) and vanilla extract and beat for 1 minute. Scrape the sides and bottom of the bowl with a spatula once again.

4. Add sieved icing sugar in four batches; mix from a low to a high speed. Scrape the sides and bottom of the bowl with a spatula and mix one more time. This is to ensure that you have no unmixed sugar in the buttercream: any unmixed sugar can get stuck in the piping nozzles and interfere with the process of piping blooms.

Neetha's Top Tips for Buttercream Brilliance

As with baking, the science of making buttercream is as important as the ingredients.

Vegetable shortening This is available in the butter section of your supermarket. Check the ingredients section for confirmation that the shortening is 70% or above vegetable fat. If it is 100% vegetable fat, it will not taste as nice. Shortening is usually advertised as being lower in fat, which makes it perfect for baking cakes. Vegetable shortening is added to stabilize the buttercream so it won't melt as easily, and will be stable enough to pipe flowers and other decorations. Avoid long-life shortening, however; only use the fresh shortening you find in the butter aisle.

Stick rigidly to the timings given for the making of the buttercream to ensure that you have the right texture of buttercream. Underbeaten buttercream will look too soft. Overbeaten buttercream will result in lots of airholes.

Always make buttercream using a **handheld electric mixer** or a **stand mixer with a K-beater**.

Once made, **always mix buttercream using a spatula** and never a beater.

If you feel your buttercream is getting too soft as you pipe, **put the piping bag in the fridge** for 10 minutes. Softening is normal as buttercream will melt due to the heat from your hands.

Once you make the buttercream, you can **use it straight away, refrigerate it for three days or freeze it for a month**. However, fresh buttercream tastes best!

Colouring your buttercream

You can use any gel colour to colour your buttercream, but avoid using liquid colours as these will thin your buttercream. Use a fresh cocktail stick (toothpick) every time you transfer colour from the bottle to the buttercream. Discard used cocktail sticks (toothpicks) and do not reinsert them into the bottle of gel as it will contaminate the colour.

For deep colours, colour your buttercream two hours ahead of decorating, as it will darken over time. See pages 22–25 for more ideas and advice on choosing and mixing buttercream colours.

A selection of gel colours and the cocktail sticks (toothpicks) that can be used to apply the gel colour to the buttercream.

Flavouring ideas

I usually pair my vanilla sponge cake with a berry compote and vanilla buttercream. Freshly-made berry compote tastes much better than shop-bought jam or conserve, but if you are short of time, by all means, you can use a bought jam or conserve.

Berry compote

INGREDIENTS

300g (10⁵⁄₈oz) berries of your choice – either one type of berry or mixed berries (you can use any berries: strawberries, raspberries, blueberries and so on); fresh or frozen

3tbsp sugar

1tbsp water

INSTRUCTIONS

1. In a medium-size saucepan, mix all the ingredients together. Bring the pan to boil over a medium heat. Keep stirring. Cook for 5 minutes or so – longer, if you are using frozen berries.

2. When the mixture is boiling and has reduced a little, you can take it off the heat and let it cool down completely.

3. You can either sieve the compote or you can use it with the 'bits' still in. I use the compote for filling a cake – either mixed with buttercream or on its own.

Chocolate buttercream

I pair my chocolate cake with chocolate buttercream. This can be used for both filling and covering the cake. Just add sieved cocoa powder (use good-quality organic cocoa) to vanilla buttercream.

There are no measurements as such: I go by the colour of the buttercream – it's up to you on how chocolatey you want your buttercream!

Add a little water or milk to loosen your buttercream if it gets too thick from the cocoa powder.

Other flavouring ideas

- You can flavour the buttercream easily by replacing the vanilla extract in the recipe with almond extract, lemon extract or orange extract, for example.

- You can add canned fruits to buttercream and use this as a filling.

- You can pair lemon curd and lemon buttercream, fruit conserves and vanilla buttercream, butterscotch or toffee sauce and vanilla or chocolate buttercream, and so on.

Cake Techniques

A solid cake structure is your blank canvas, which is vital to master before you dive into the artistry of working with buttercream.

Covering the cake

Achieving perfectly-covered cakes is one of the most discussed topics in my classes; as I tell my students, covering a cake flawlessly takes more skill and practice then it does to paint or pipe flowers, so be patient with yourself. Each and every step detailed is vital, so do please follow them all thoroughly.

Step 1 - Preparing cake layers

A perfectly-covered cake has even layers of cake underneath: this is an important element that we often forget. If for any reason you have an uneven bake, or browned edges, use a cake leveller to level the cake, as demonstrated below.

The photographs below show how to cut and level a cake in half. Repeat the steps to cut your cake into quarter-deep layers.

1

2

1. Lay the cake on a flat surface. Adjust the height of the wire in the cake leveller to your desired height.

2. Slide the cake leveller through the cake to cut even layers.

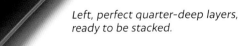

Left, perfect quarter-deep layers, ready to be stacked.

Step 2 – Filling and stacking your cake

If it's a small cake or single-tier cake you are making, you can use glossy cake cards on which to stack your cake. If you are creating a multi-tiered cake or a heavy cake, a cake drum is a better choice.

1

2

3

1. Put a dollop of buttercream in the middle of the cake drum before placing your cake layer on top. This will ensure that the cake sticks to the cake drum during any transportation. If you would like your cake to be extra secure, you can use some melted chocolate or ganache to stick the bottom layer of cake to the cake card or drum.

2. Use a piping bag filled with your chosen filling and pipe an even amount of the filling over the first of the cake layers. Use a spatula to spread the filling evenly over the cake layer.

3. Stack the next cake layer on top and repeat the process.

Step 3 – Crumb coating

Crumb coating is the process of applying a thin layer of buttercream all around the cake. This is an important process because the buttercream layer will secure all the crumbs so that they don't get in the way when you come to cover the cake. A very thin layer of buttercream is all you need. Use a palette knife to apply the crumb coating – it is as simple as applying a layer of butter to your toast!

1. Push any excess buttercream between the cake layers into the cake to ensure there are no gaps.

2. Pipe evenly-spaced strands of buttercream on the top and around the cake.

3. Using a palette knife, spread this evenly over the cake.

4. Run a cake smoother around the cake to catch all the excess buttercream. All you need is a thin layer of buttercream.

5. Remove all excess buttercream into a bowl. Note: Don't reuse this buttercream to cover your cake as this buttercream may have cake crumbs in.

6. Repeat the same process on the top of the cake as well.

7. Let the crumb-coated cake rest for at least 30 minutes.

Step 4 – Covering and smoothing the cake

To cover the cake, the trick is to have an even layer of buttercream all over. The easiest way to achieve this is by piping rings of buttercream around and on top of the cake. Finally, you can use a smoother to smooth the buttercream in sections.

Ensure that you don't rush this process: lots of practice in applying the correct techniques will help you master the 'smoothing technique' in no time!

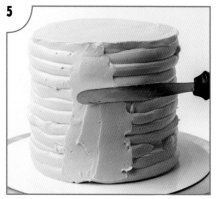

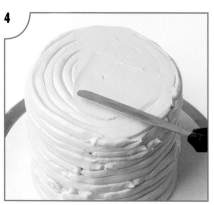

1. Apply an even layer of buttercream all around the cake, starting on the top. You can use a piping bag with a fine hole cut at the end to do this.

2. Work in a spiral motion to cover the whole top of the cake.

3. Move down to pipe around the side of the cake. Rotate your cake board or turntable and pipe in a continuous motion.

4. Smooth the top of the cake with the palette knife.

5. Smooth down the side of the cake with the palette knife in the same way.

6. Place a cake smoother against the cake and slowly smooth one section at a time. Begin at the top of the cake.

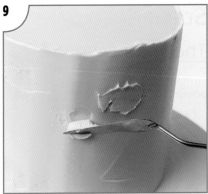

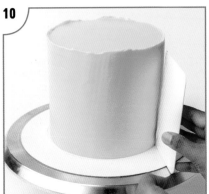

7. Scrape and smooth around the side of the cake with the cake smoother.

8. You can scrape off the excess buttercream from the smoother using a tapered palette knife.

9. Use the excess to fill in any obvious gaps in the cake covering.

10. Repeat steps 6–9 until the cake is smooth.

11. Smooth the top of the cake again, using the tapered palette knife. Scrape off any excess onto the smoother again, and decant into a container.

The covered cake.

Stacking the cake

The importance of dowels

I use dowels – thin, cylindrical lengths of wood or plastic – to ensure that the bottom cake tier holds the weight of the top cake tiers.

I am using four dowels for this two-tier cake, *Birds and Blooms*, shown on pages 102–107. If your cake has three tiers or more, you can add six or eight dowels to the bottom, biggest cake tier to ensure that it bears all the weight of the top tiers.

It is a good idea to freeze the covered cake tiers before stacking them, so that the cake stays intact.

The dowels ensure that the bottom tier supports the top tier of the cake.

1. Insert a dowel all the way into the cake.

2. Use a little buttercream to mark where the dowel reaches the top of the cake, then take out the dowel slowly.

3. Cut a total of four dowels of the same length (height).

4. Insert the dowels into the cake. Ensure that they are within the circumference of the top-tier cake. The idea is that the top-tier cake can sit comfortably on the dowels.

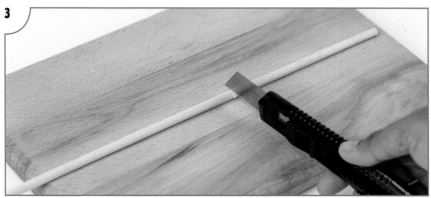
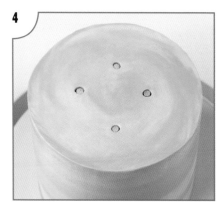

Covering cupcakes

1. Using some buttercream in a piping bag with a fine hole at the end, pipe a strand of buttercream to cover the top of the cupcake.

2. Use a palette knife to smooth the buttercream.

Buttercream Techniques

Adding gel colours to buttercream

1

2

3

4
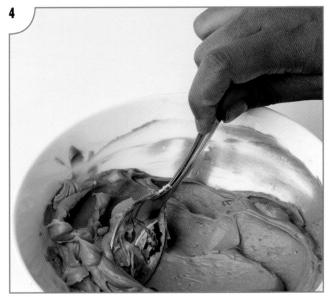

1. Use a clean cocktail stick (toothpick) to transfer the gel colour.

2. Transfer the gel colour into the buttercream.

3. Use a spoon or spatula to mix the gel colour well with the buttercream.

4. Always start with a little gel colour: you can add more if need be. Remember to use a fresh cocktail stick (toothpick) each time, to avoid contaminating your original gel colour.

Choosing buttercream colours

The right colour combination plays a huge part in your cake-designing process. We often overlook this area, but I highly recommend you invest some time here – I promise you will reap the rewards.

Inspiration for colour combinations is everywhere – look for pretty dresses, floral homeware, wallpapers, greetings cards. It is all about finding colour combinations that appeal to you and reinventing them as cake designs.

COLOUR COMBINATIONS THAT WORK

Understanding the basic colour wheel will help you decide the best colour combinations for your cake. In a colour wheel, you will see primary, secondary and tertiary colours, as follows.

THE BASIC COLOUR WHEEL

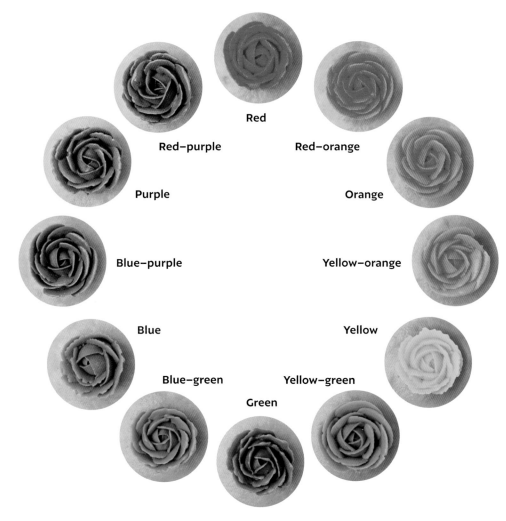

Red

Red–purple

Red–orange

Purple

Orange

Blue–purple

Yellow–orange

Blue

Yellow

Blue–green

Yellow–green

Green

Primary colours

Red, yellow and blue are the primary colours.

Secondary colours

These are the colours achieved by mixing equal amounts of two primary colours:

• Orange = red + yellow

• Purple = red + blue

• Green = yellow + blue.

Tertiary colours

These are the colours that fall between, and are mixed from, the primary and secondary colours:

• Red–purple

• Blue–purple

• Blue–green

• Yellow–green

• Yellow–orange

• Red–orange.

COMPLEMENTARY COLOURS

Complementary colours sit opposite each other in the colour wheel – for example, red and green, and yellow and purple. If you are looking for bold cake designs, choose complementary colours as they will create contrast and have a striking effect on your design.

ANALOGOUS COLOURS

These are the colours that are right next to each other on the colour wheel – for example, yellow, yellow-orange and orange. When these colours are used together, they give a harmonious look to your design.

COMPOUND COLOURS

Compound colours comprise two adjacent colours in the colour wheel and one colour opposite on the colour wheel. for example – red–orange, red and green. Compound colours are very much like complementary colours in that they create a striking contrast, but having two adjacent colours from the colour wheel creates a smoother transition.

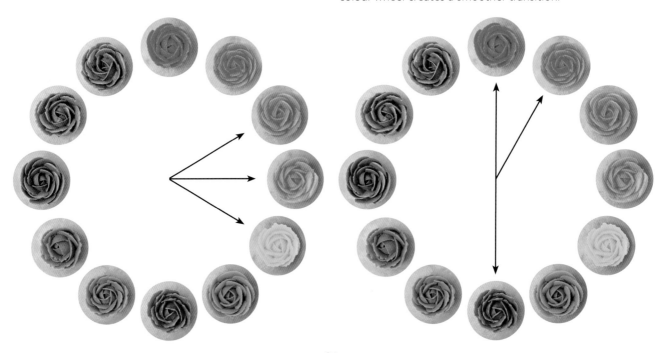

TRIAD AND TETRAD COLOURS

If you would like a colourful cake, perhaps a triad or tetrad colour combination is the best way forward. Triad colours are evenly spaced on the colour wheel in the form of a triangle – for example, yellow, blue and red, or purple, orange and green.

Tetrad colours are evenly spaced on the colour wheel in the form of a square – for example, yellow, purple, blue–green and red–orange.

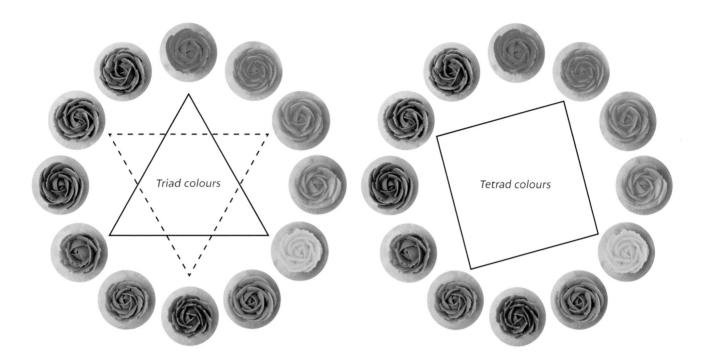

Triad colours

Tetrad colours

POPULAR COLOURS

When you mix two or more gel colours, a little magic happens to transform the colour dramatically so you can achieve the perfect red, burgundy or even black! Below are some of my favourite colour combinations:

- Black – chocolate buttercream + black gel colour;
- White – uncoloured buttercream + white gel colour;
- Brown – chocolate buttercream;
- Red – mostly red + a little orange + a little dot of black;
- Avocado – green + yellow + a dot of ivory;
- Burgundy – pink + a little purple;
- Plum – violet + a little red;
- Navy blue – blue + a little violet;
- Raspberry – pink + a little red.

A dot of ivory will help to decrease the brightness of any colour; a dot of black will help darken the colour. I tend to use a neutral colour like cream or white with my complementary colours to tone down the contrast a little.

Preparing your piping bags

Preparing your piping bags is an art in itself. You can achieve realistic-looking colour combinations for your flowers by layering multiple colours in one piping bag.

Attaching a coupler

A coupler is a small, clever tool which, when paired with a piping bag, enables us to change the nozzles without having to change the whole piping bag. Here, I show you how it works.

Scissors, piping bag, nozzle and coupler.

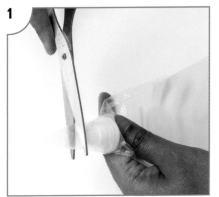

1. Put the bottom part of the coupler onto the piping bag. Cut the piping bag just above the rim of the coupler.

2. Attach the nozzle of your choice to the coupler.

3. Screw on the top part of the coupler to secure the nozzle. Tighten the coupler, making sure that the edge of the nozzle is in line with the edge of the piping bag. This will make the layering of colours easier, which we will see on pages 28–29.

Filling your piping bag

1

1. Place your prepared piping bag inside a tall cup or glass, ready to be filled.

2

2. For a single colour, all you need to do is fill the piping bag with your coloured buttercream, using a spoon to decant the buttercream. Fill no more than half of the piping bag.

3

3. Filling only half – or less – of the piping bag with buttercream will ensure that you have a good grip when piping.

Filling your piping bag for two-tone piping

For realistic flower piping, it is a great idea to prepare two-tone piping bags. Here, I have used orange and yellow buttercream.

Prepare two piping bags with coloured buttercream, ready for layering. Place a third, empty piping bag flat on your work area with a nozzle and coupler attached. Ensure that the edge of the nozzle is in line with the edge of the empty piping bag.

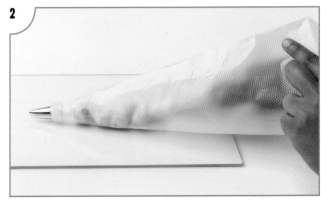

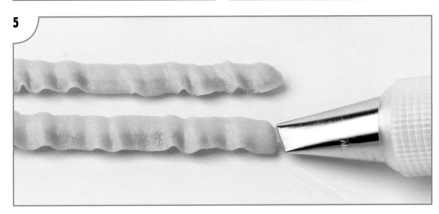

1. Using one of the coloured buttercreams – orange in this example – pipe an even strand of buttercream along the inside edge of the piping bag.

2. Using the second coloured buttercream, yellow in this example, pipe more buttercream on top of the first layer.

3. Pick up the now-full piping bag and hold it vertically.

4. Using your fingers, squeeze the buttercream so that the two colours are lightly blended together.

5. Now you can start piping. You will see the two shades of coloured buttercream are lightly blended where they meet.

Filling your piping bag for multi-tone piping

You can layer more colours – three or four – to create multi-tone piping bags. Prepare three or more piping bags with coloured buttercream, ready for layering. Here, I have used purple, blue and uncoloured buttercream.

Place a fourth, empty, piping bag flat on your work area, with nozzle and coupler attached. Ensure that the edge of the nozzle is in line with the edge of the piping bag.

1

2

3

4

5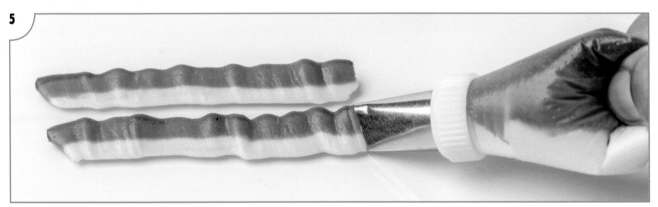

1. Using one of the piping bags – containing uncoloured buttercream in this example – pipe an even strand of buttercream along the inside edge of the empty piping bag.

2. Using the second coloured buttercream – blue in this example – pipe more buttercream on top of the first layer.

3. Using the third coloured buttercream – purple in this example – pipe more buttercream on top of the second layer.

4. Pick up the piping bag and hold it vertically. Using your fingers, squeeze the buttercream so that the three colours are lightly blended together.

5. Now you can start piping. You will see the three shades of coloured buttercream are lightly blended where they meet.

Preparing to pipe a flower

PREPARING A FLOWER NAIL

Cut a square of greaseproof paper to sit on top of the flower nail – you can then pipe your buttercream flowers onto the flower nail, to be transferred to a tray for freezing, or directly onto your cake.

You can also use a customized wooden block with a fine hole drilled into the top – this block supports the flower nail, allowing you to add details to the flower, freehand.

Piping bag of buttercream, flower nail, block and greaseproof paper.

1

2

3

4

1. Apply some buttercream directly onto the flower nail.

2. Stick a greaseproof paper square onto the flower nail.

3. Your flower nail is ready to be used to support your piped flowers.

4. Once you have piped your flower onto the flower nail, you can rest the nail in a wooden block to support it as you add final details.

Palette-knife painting techniques

These are artists' palette knives that we are using for our painting: you can source these from any art store. You can use a different-sized palette knife depending on the size of the flower that you'd like to paint. Here, I am using a small palette knife – size 1 – to paint a chrysanthemum (see also page 56).

Decant your buttercream onto a flat surface such as a plastic chopping board or glass tray to do your painting.

Loading your palette knife and painting petals

1

2

3

4

5

1. Using a palette knife, pick up some buttercream. The amount of buttercream you pick up will determine the thickness of the petal that you are going to paint.

2. Apply it back onto the tray: this is the first step of the smoothing process.

3. Pick up the buttercream again, using the side of the palette knife.

4. You will see that the buttercream on the back of the palette knife is much smoother now. Smooth buttercream ensures that you can paint a well-defined petal, with clean edges.

5. You can now start painting by applying this buttercream firmly to the surface and gently sliding your palette knife inwards to create a petal or leaf shape.

The Buttercream Flowers

Piped flowers

Drop flowers,
pages 34–35

Sunflower,
page 36

Cherry blossoms,
page 37

Poinsettia,
pages 38–39

Hydrangea,
pages 40–41

Helenium
'Ruby Tuesday',
pages 42–43

Begonia,
page 44

Gladiolus,
page 45

Chrysanthemum,
pages 46–47

Rose,
pages 48–49

Peony,
page 50

Daisy,
page 51

Piped leaves

pages 52–55

Painted flowers

Chrysanthemum,
page 56

Daisy,
page 57

Aster,
page 58

Cherry blossoms,
page 59

Icelandic poppy,
page 60

Rose,
page 61

Drop flowers, piped

These are really simple, beginner-friendly flowers. You can use this same technique in a different colour, like blue or pink for example, to create the appearance of a small hydrangea. These drop flowers are great filler flowers for big cakes, as well as cupcakes.

The drop flowers are piped using orange buttercream here; for the leaves, fill a piping bag with green buttercream. For the centre of the flower, you can use a brown (chocolate) buttercream in a piping bag with a fine hole cut at the end, or alternatively a Wilton 2 writing nozzle (see page 36).

The Wilton 224 nozzle, used for the petals.

The Wilton 352 nozzle, used for the leaves.

1

2

3

4

1. Prepare a flower nail with a greaseproof paper square (see page 30). Hold the piping bag perpendicular to the flower nail and squeeze a circle of buttercream.

2. Pipe the buttercream evenly to fill the circle.

3. This is the base of the flower cluster: you can make this base bigger or smaller, as you would like.

4. Place the nozzle to lightly touch the base and apply an even pressure to release a good amount of buttercream. As the petals start to form, gently lift up the nozzle to let the petals flare out. Now stop piping and gently tap the middle of the flower to attach all the petals in place. Gently take away the nozzle.

5

6

7

8

9

5. Pipe small drop flowers all over the base.

6. Pipe more small drop flowers inside the base. This forms the first layer of flowers.

7. Now pipe more drop flowers over the first layer of flowers to create a domed effect.

8. Using brown buttercream in a piping bag with a fine hole cut at the end, pipe small dots in the centres of the drop flowers.

9. Using a piping bag with green buttercream and a Wilton 352 nozzle, pipe simple leaves in between the flowers (see page 52). For this technique, place one of the sharp edges of the nozzle in between the flowers and apply light pressure to release a very small amount of buttercream. Stop piping and gently pull the nozzle away to form a tapered leaf. This completes your drop flower arrangement.

Sunflower, piped

Sunflowers are also great, beginner-friendly flowers that are beautiful and easy to pipe.

For the centre of the sunflower, you can use both a light and dark shade of brown (chocolate) buttercream each in a separate piping bag, either with a fine hole cut at the end, or with a Wilton 2 writing nozzle attached. For the petals, you can use a yellow buttercream.

The Wilton 2 writing nozzle, used for the outline of the flower centre.

The Wilton 352 nozzle, used for the petals.

1

2

3

4

5

1. Using the brown buttercream, pipe a circle in the middle of the flower nail.

2. To pipe the petals, place your nozzle at a 30° angle, with one of the sharp edges of the nozzle touching the flower nail. Applying firm pressure, pipe a good amount of buttercream to form a sturdy base. Move your nozzle outwards from the centre circle, applying even pressure. When the petal reaches your desired length, stop piping and gently pull away the nozzle to form a tapered end.

3. Pipe more petals around the circle to complete the first layer, then pipe a second layer of petals, positioning each petal between two petals on the first layer.

4. Use brown buttercream to fill the middle of the flower.

5. Finally, using both light and dark shades of brown buttercream, pipe tiny dots to form the middle of the sunflower.

Cherry blossoms, piped

Cherry blossoms symbolize renewal as they bloom at the beginning of spring. This simple blooms come in hues of white, pink and yellow – so delicate and utterly beautiful.

These cherry blossoms are created using the two-tone piping method again, explained on page 28, in tones of pink and white; red buttercream is used to create the flower centre.

The Wilton 103 nozzle, used for the petals.

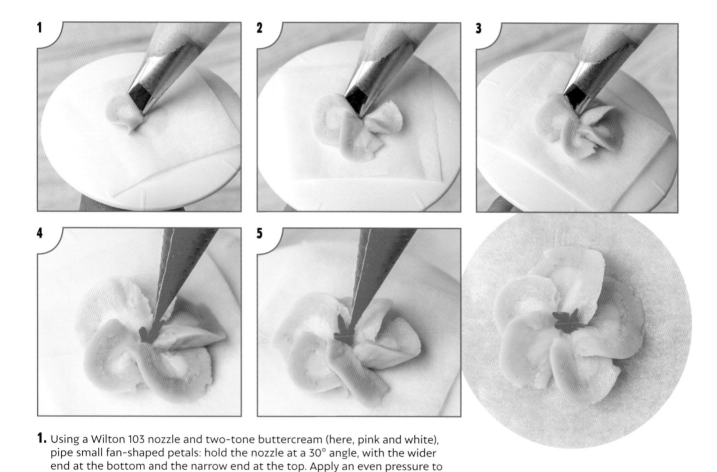

1. Using a Wilton 103 nozzle and two-tone buttercream (here, pink and white), pipe small fan-shaped petals: hold the nozzle at a 30° angle, with the wider end at the bottom and the narrow end at the top. Apply an even pressure to pipe each petal.

2. Pipe more fan-shaped petals, each time placing the nozzle below the petal previously piped.

3. Pipe five petals altogether.

4. Using a piping bag with a fine hole cut at the end, begin to pipe strands of red buttercream in the middle of the flower.

5. Pipe three strands in total. This completes the cherry blossom.

Poinsettia, piped

Poinsettia flowers are a great choice for Christmas-themed cakes and cupcakes. I usually choose bright red or ivory buttercream for poinsettias, and pipe the flowers using a leaf nozzle such as the Wilton 352. Here, we are piping the petals in red buttercream.

For the centre of the flower, you can use a brown (chocolate) buttercream and a yellow buttercream for the final detailing on the flower centre. Both can be piped with a Wilton 2 writing nozzle, or a piping bag with a fine hole cut at the end.

The Wilton 352 leaf nozzle, used for the petals.

The Wilton 2 writing nozzle, used for the flower centre.

The Wilton 2 writing nozzle, here used for the tips on the centre of the flower.

1

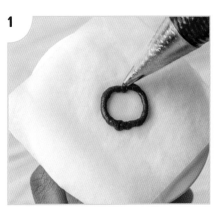

2

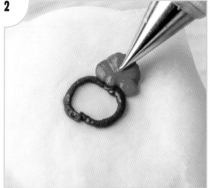

3

4

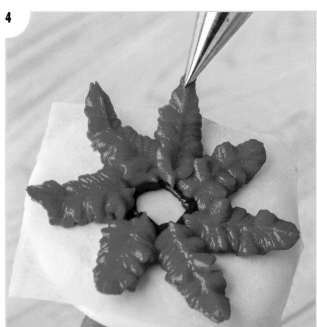

1. Using the brown buttercream, pipe a circle in the middle of the flower nail.

2. Place the nozzle at a 30° angle with one of the pointed sides of the nozzle touching the flower nail. Apply gentle pressure and lightly move the nozzle back and forth to achieve a wavy petal.

3. When you reach the desired length of your petal, stop piping and pull the nozzle away to form a tapered end.

4. Pipe similar petals all around the circle. This is the first layer of petals.

5

6

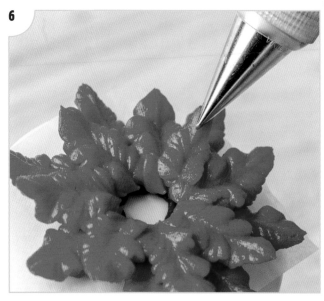

7

8

9

5. Now pipe a second layer of petals between pairs of the petals that you have already piped. Make sure to pipe petals of slightly varying lengths.

6. Now pipe a third layer of smaller petals.

7. Using the brown buttercream, fill the centre of the flower.

8. Pipe small dots of buttercream over the centre.

9. Then, finally, using yellow buttercream, pipe tiny tips in between the brown dots to complete your poinsettia.

Hydrangea, piped

Hydrangeas are stunning globes of small flowers that usually come in hues of pink, blue and purple, and sometimes in white and pale green. The hydrangea is beautiful piped as a cluster of flowers or as a filler flower on cakes.

Here, we are applying the two-tone piping technique explained on page 28, with purple and pink buttercreams, to create the petals of the hydrangea. You will also need to prepare a piping bag of uncoloured buttercream in a piping bag with a fine hole cut at the end, for the flower centre details.

The Wilton 103 nozzle, used for the petals.

The Wilton 352 nozzle, used for the leaves.

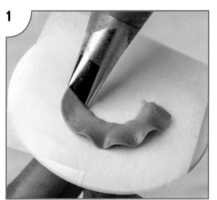

1. Using the Wilton 103 nozzle and two-tone, purple–pink buttercream, pipe a ring of the buttercream. This will determine the size of the hydrangea globe.

2. Fill the ring with buttercream, in a spiral motion.

3. Pipe more buttercream in the middle to create some height, forming a dome.

4. Place the nozzle against one side of the dome. Choose a central point for the flower; place the wider end of the nozzle there and the narrow end of the nozzle facing outwards. Apply gentle pressure to release fan-shaped petals. Pipe four petals around the central point to form a small flower.

5. Similarly, pipe more four-petal flowers around the dome-like structure.

6. You can pipe more flowers on top of the dome.

7. Once you have piped flowers all over the dome, you can pipe individual petals to fill any gaps.

8. Using a piping bag with a fine hole cut at the end and some uncoloured buttercream, pipe dots in the middle of the flowers.

9. Finally, using some green buttercream and a Wilton 352 nozzle, pipe small leaves in between the flowers (see page 52 for guidance on piping simple leaves). Place the nozzle ever so gently in between any gaps and apply a little pressure to release a small leaf.

Helenium 'Ruby Tuesday', piped

This helenium is a beautiful flower that comes in hues of red, yellow and orange. We are making a heart-shaped petal stroke with which to pipe this gorgeous flower.

For the centre of the flower, you can use brown (chocolate) buttercream in a piping bag either with a fine hole cut at the end, or a Wilton 2 writing nozzle. The helenium petals are piped using petal-shaped nozzles – you can use any size nozzle depending on the size of the flower you intend to pipe. I have used a Wilton 104 nozzle.

For the centre detailing of the flower, you can use yellow buttercream in a piping bag with Wilton 1 or 2 writing nozzle or, again, a piping bag with a fine hole cut at the end.

The Wilton 2 writing nozzle, used for the flower centre outline.

The Wilton 104 nozzle, used for the petals.

The Wilton 2 writing nozzle, here used for the stamens.

1

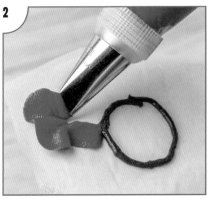
2

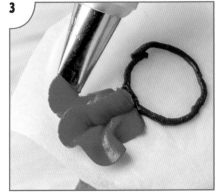
3

1. Using brown buttercream, pipe a circle in the middle of your flower nail.

2. To pipe heart-shaped petals, place the nozzle on the circle with the wider end of the nozzle at the bottom and the narrow end at the top. Squeeze the piping bag gently and pull up to the desired length of the petal. Lightly bring the nozzle downwards, creating the dip on the top of the petal, like a heart.

3. Rotate the nozzle 180° and squeeze the piping bag gently to pipe the other half of the petal, bringing the nozzle downwards this time.

4. Pipe heart-shaped petals all the way around the circle. Always start a new petal underneath the petal already piped to ensure that you do not squash any piped petals.

5. Using brown buttercream, fill the middle of the circle

6. Hold the nozzle perpendicular in the middle of the circle. Applying an even pressure, squeeze out a good amount of buttercream to form a dome.

7. Pipe tiny strands of brown buttercream all over the dome. Make sure to create a good base so that the tiny strands hold their shape and don't fall off.

8. Pipe tiny dots of yellow buttercream on top of the brown strands. Repeat until you have added detailing to the entire flower centre. Your helenium is complete.

Begonia, piped

Begonias have layers and layers of gorgeous ruffled petals that come in a variety of colours – here, we are piping a pale pink begonia. This is also a beginner-friendly flower and can be piped in various sizes.

This beautiful summer bloom is perfect for any colourful floral cake.

The Wilton 104 nozzle, used for the petals.

The Wilton 233 nozzle, used for the stamens.

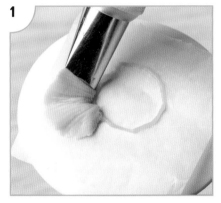

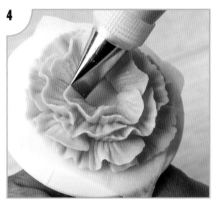

1. Using yellow buttercream and a Wilton 3 nozzle (or a piping bag with a fine hole cut at the end), pipe a guide circle for the middle of the flower. Using the pink buttercream with a Wilton 104 nozzle, pipe curved, ruffled petals: place the nozzle on the guide circle at a 30° angle, with the wider end of the nozzle on the guide circle and the narrow end of the nozzle facing outwards. Apply gentle pressure, lightly moving the nozzle up and down, and move the nozzle around the circle to release a ruffled petal.

2. Pipe similar ruffled petals, positioning the nozzle halfway down the top of the petals already piped. Complete the first layer of petals.

3. Pipe a second layer of petals, positioning the nozzle inside the guide circle so you can see a little of the layer of petals already piped.

4. Pipe similar overlapping petals, completing the second layer, and repeat for a third layer of petals.

5. Finally, using yellow buttercream and a Wilton 233 nozzle, hold the nozzle upright in the middle of the flower and squeeze evenly to pipe stamens.

Gladiolus, piped

Gladiolus is a stunning tropical flower that resembles a lily or hibiscus. Together, these flowers are quite dramatic and can take the central position on any cake arrangement.

The petals are formed in red buttercream; the flower centre in yellow, with brown (chocolate) buttercream for the last details.

The Wilton 104 nozzle, used for the petals.

1

2

3

4

5

6

1. Using yellow buttercream in a piping bag with a fine hole cut at the end, pipe and fill a guide circle for the middle of the flower.

2. Using a Wilton 104 nozzle and red buttercream, pipe a leaf-shaped petal: place the nozzle at a 30° angle with the wider end of the nozzle at the bottom and the narrow end at the top. Squeeze the piping bag gently in a wavy motion and pull up to the desired length of the petal. Rotate the nozzle and squeeze the piping bag gently, again in a wavy motion, to pipe the other half of the petal, bringing the nozzle downwards this time.

3. Pipe two more petals, equally spaced from each other, as if to form the three points of a triangle.

4. Pipe three more petals in between the petals already piped.

5. Using the yellow buttercream again, pipe 1cm- (³⁄₈in-) long stamens in the middle of the flower.

6. Finally, using brown (chocolate) buttercream in a piping bag with a fine hole cut at the end, pipe small dots at the tip of the stamens for further detailing.

Chrysanthemum, piped

The chrysanthemum has a multitude of petals and hence is an intricate flower to pipe, but the results are absolutely stunning.

I tend to pipe my chrysanthemums using two separate shades of buttercream: usually a lighter shade for the outer petals and a darker shade for the inner petals. This creates a visually striking, realistic look.

The WIlton 81 nozzle, used with both colours of buttercream.

1

2

3

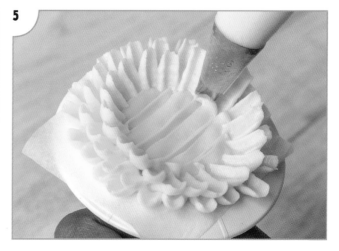

4

5

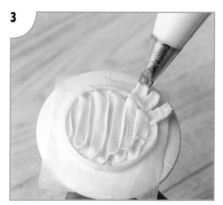

1. Using a Wilton 81 nozzle, pipe a ring in the lighter shade of buttercream. This will determine the size of the flower.

2. Fill the ring with buttercream – this forms the base for your flower.

3. Place the nozzle at a 30° angle, with the curved side of the nozzle facing inwards. Apply gentle pressure to release a good amount of buttercream. Make sure the base of the petal is strong, then move the nozzle upwards, applying even pressure. When the petal reaches the desired length, stop piping and pull away gently.

4. Pipe similar petals next to each other, all around the base.

5. Now pipe the second layer of petals, making sure there are no gaps between the adjacent petals or between each layer of petals.

6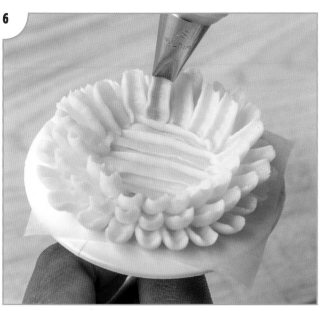

7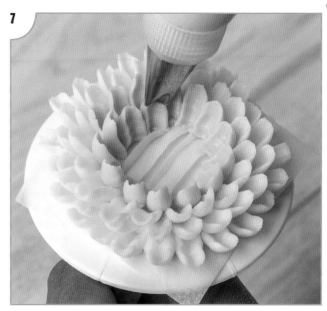

8

9

6. After piping three layers of petals using the lighter-coloured buttercream, pipe more layers using the darker tone of buttercream.

7. Repeat the same processes to add more layers of petals, again making sure there are no gaps between the adjacent petals as well as between each layer.

8. As you reach the centre of the flower, position the nozzle perpendicular to the flower nail.

9. Finish off the flower by piping two petals facing each other. This is the centremost point of the flower.

Rose, piped

The rose is an absolutely beautiful buttercream flower. It is an advanced flower – quite three-dimensional – so I advise that you practise it many times until you get the hang of it.

Here, I have used bright red and ivory buttercreams to pipe the roses, using petal nozzles. You can use any size petal nozzle, depending on the size of the rose you intend to pipe. I have used a Wilton 104 nozzle for the smaller – red – rose; you can use a Wilton 125 for a larger rose, such as the ivory rose shown on the opposite page.

The Wilton 104 nozzle, used for the petals of the smaller rose.

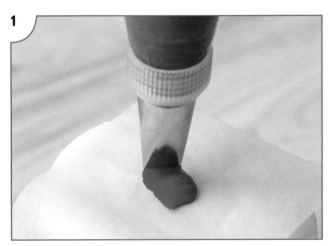

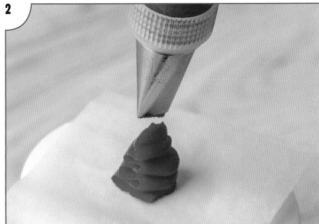

1. Prepare a flower nail with a greaseproof paper square on top (see page 30). Hold the nozzle vertical to the flower nail.

2. Squeeze out an even amount of buttercream to form a cone in the middle of the flower nail. Make sure the base is sturdy and the top tapered.

3. Pipe a first, curved upright petal to wrap around the cone.

4. Pipe a second petal, starting from the middle of the petal already piped.

5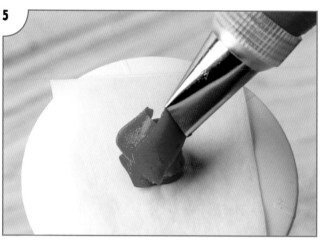

6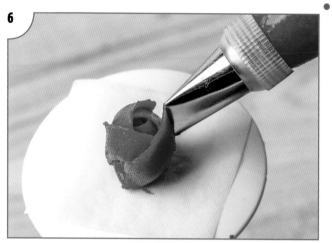

7

8

9

5. Pipe more petals to wrap the cone completely, revealing only a small hole in the middle of the cluster of petals, which forms the bud of the rose.

6. Pipe more curved petals around the rose.

7. As you reach the third layer of petals, slowly turn your nozzle to face outwards so the petals are piped as if the rose is blooming.

8. Pipe more layers of petals.

9. Pipe as many layers as you'd like depending on the size of the rose you'd like to create.

A larger variation on the piped rose.

Peony, piped

Peonies are very similar to roses, but they have more closed-off petals. They appear as huge fluffy blooms, which never fail to create a dramatic effect on any floral design.

The petals of the peony are piped using the two-tone piping method explained on page 28, in yellow and pink buttercreams.

The Wilton 233 nozzle, used for the flower centre.

A JEM 121 nozzle, used for the petals. You could also use a Wilton 125 nozzle.

1

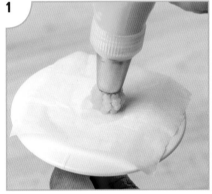

2

3

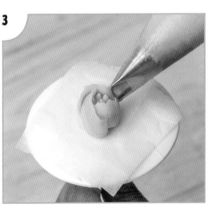

4

5

1. Using yellow buttercream and a Wilton 233 nozzle, pipe the central stamen of the flowers.

2. Using two-tone buttercream in yellow and pink, with a JEM 121 nozzle, pipe closed petals all around the central structure. Place the nozzle flat against the centre with the wider end of the nozzle at the bottom and narrow end at the top. Pipe curved upright petals.

3. Pipe three similar petals all around the centre, making sure you can see the stamens ever so slightly. This is the bud.

4. Pipe more closed upright curved petals all around the bud of the peony.

5. You can pipe more layers depending on the size of the flower you want to create; you can also use the same techniques to pipe different-sized peonies.

Daisy, piped

Daisies are such beautiful delicate flowers that symbolize innocence, purity and love. They are easy to pipe in buttercream and work well on their own or as filler flowers on your cake designs.

The PME 32R nozzle, used for the petals. You could also use a Wilton 81 nozzle.

The WIlton 2 writing nozzle, used to pipe the centre of the flower.

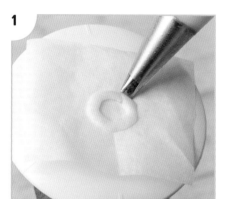

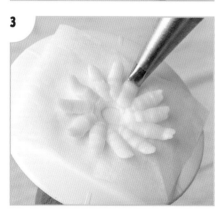

1. Using a PME 32R nozzle and some white buttercream, pipe a small circle, which is going to be the middle of the flower.

2. Touching the nozzle to the ring of piped buttercream, apply gentle and even pressure to release pulled petals. Once you reach the desired length, stop piping and pull away.

3. Pipe petals all around the ring of buttercream, making sure there are no gaps between the petals.

4. Pipe a second layer of petals, placing the nozzle between two petals already piped.

5. Finally, using a writing nozzle and some yellow buttercream, pipe small dots in the middle of the flower.

Piped leaves

Piped leaves are not just to beautify the cake design; they support the flowers from underneath to ensure they stay in place once the cake is decorated.

   You can create different looks for your leaves using just two kinds of nozzle. The leaves on this page have been created using the Wilton 352 nozzle.

You can create the first three leaves using a nozzle such as the Wilton 352 – just look for the fish mouth!

Simple leaf

Place the nozzle at a 30° angle with one of the sharp ends of the nozzle touching the surface. Apply gentle pressure to release a good amount of buttercream. When the leaf gets to the desired length, stop piping, and gently pull away the nozzle to create a nice, tapered tip.

The simple leaves in place on the Sunset Beauty *cake – see pages 86–89.*

Ruffled leaf

Place the nozzle at a 30° angle, with one of the sharp ends of the nozzle touching the surface. Again, apply gentle pressure to release a good amount of buttercream, this time in a wavy (to-and-fro) motion. When the leaf gets to the desired length, stop piping and gently pull away the nozzle to create a tapered tip.

The ruffled leaves being piped in place on the Summer Basket *arrangement – see pages 80–85.*

Ivy leaf

Pipe two simple leaves facing each other at a small angle. Finish off by piping one simple leaf in the middle.

Pipe three of these leaves close together to give the impression of a holly leaf. These leaves feature on the Christmas Cupcake Wreath – see pages 72–79.

The completed piped leaves.

More leaves

Create these three leaves using the Wilton 102 nozzle or any similar petal-shaped nozzle. Use a Wilton 103 or 104 for larger leaves.

The Wilton 102 nozzle, used to pipe the leaves on these pages.

Simple leaf

Place the nozzle at a 30° angle with the wide end of the nozzle at the bottom and the narrow end at the top. Squeeze the piping bag gently and pull up to the desired length of the leaf. Rotate the nozzle and squeeze the piping bag gently to pipe the other half of the leaf, bringing the nozzle downwards this time.

The simple leaves being piped onto the Majestic Beauty cake – see pages 120–127.

Ruffled leaf

Place the nozzle at a 30° angle with the wide end of the nozzle at the bottom and the narrow end at the top. Squeeze the piping bag gently, in a wavy motion, and pull up to the desired length of the leaf. Rotate the nozzle and squeeze the piping bag gently, again in a wavy motion, to pipe the other half of the leaf, bringing the nozzle downwards this time.

The ruffled leaves in place on the Tropical Petal Cascade cake – see pages 114–119.

Group of leaves

Start off by piping one simple leaf (see opposite). Then carry on working down an invisible line, piping more simple leaves on either side.

This kind of leaf pattern would suit a larger, two- or three-tiered, cake design.

The completed piped leaves.

Chrysanthemum, painted

Chrysanthemums are one of the easiest kinds of flowers to paint with buttercream. The size of the palette knife that you use will determine the size of the chrysanthemum.

Buttercreams in pale pink, dark pink and green; small palette knife; yellow buttercream in a piping bag with a fine hole cut at the top.

1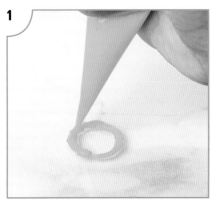

2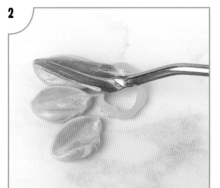

3

4

5

1. Using yellow buttercream in a piping bag with a fine hole cut at the end, pipe a circle: this will be the middle of the chrysanthemum.

2. Using a small palette knife, pick up some buttercream (see page 31). Place the palette knife flat on the surface and gently pull the palette knife inwards in one clean stroke. Paint petals all around the piped circle.

3. Once you have painted the first layer of petals, start the second layer. Using a darker shade of pink buttercream, paint similar petals as a second layer. Place the palette knife flat between two petals that you have already painted. Gently pull the palette knife inwards in one clean stroke, making sure not to squash any painted petals. Paint more petals all around.

4. Using the yellow buttercream in a piping bag, pipe small dots in the middle of the chrysanthemum.

5. Finally, using the small palette knife with green buttercream, paint in some narrow leaves in the same manner as you have painted the petals. See Tip, right.

Tip

The easiest way to paint leaves once your flower is painted is by going under the painted petals and slowly bringing the buttercream outwards.

Daisy, painted

These painted daisies are beginner-friendly: the strokes are clean and simple, similar to the chrysanthemums, opposite.

Buttercreams in white and green; small palette knife; yellow buttercream in a piping bag with a fine hole cut at the top.

1
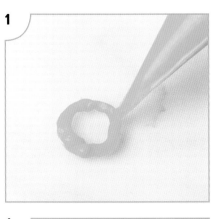

2

3

4

5

6

1. Using yellow buttercream in a piping bag, pipe a circle for the middle of the daisy.

2. Using a small palette knife, pick up some buttercream (see page 31). Place the palette knife flat on the surface and gently pull the palette knife inwards in one clean stroke.

3. In a similar fashion, paint petals all around the piped circle.

4. Using the yellow buttercream in a piping bag, pipe small dots all around the edge of the piped circle.

5. Pipe more dots to fill the middle of the daisy.

6. Using a small palette knife and some green buttercream, paint in some leaves as you would paint petals; see opposite for a tip on how to paint a leaf underneath a painted petal.

Aster, painted

Painting an aster is very much like painting a daisy (see page 57). To paint the side view of an aster, you simply need to create a semi-circle.

You will need a cocktail stick (toothpick) to create texture on the leaves.

Buttercreams in purple and green; small palette knife; yellow buttercream in a piping bag with a fine hole cut at the top.

1. Using a small palette knife, pick up some buttercream (see page 31). Place the palette knife flat on the surface and gently pull the palette knife inwards in one clean stroke. Paint petals all around in a circle.

2. Using yellow buttercream in a piping bag, pipe small dots in the flower centre.

3. Pipe more dots to add height, and create a dome.

4. To paint the side view of an aster, paint narrow petals in a semi-circle. Pipe small dots on top of the semi-circle, again in a dome shape.

5. Using a small palette knife, pick up some green buttercream and paint leaves as you would paint narrow petals.

6. Add detailing to the leaves with a cocktail stick (toothpick).

Cherry blossoms, painted

Cherry blossoms feature broad, wavy petals and hence they require a different kind of stroke with the palette knife. This is an intermediate flower, so I advise that you attempt it once you are fully comfortable with painting chrysanthemums (see page 56).

Buttercreams in orange and green; small palette knife; red buttercream in a piping bag with a fine hole cut at the top.

1
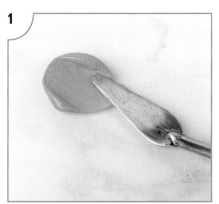

2

3

4

5

1. Using a small palette knife, pick up some orange buttercream (see page 31). Place the palette knife flat on the surface and gently move the knife to one side in a wavy motion to create a broad ruffled petal.

2. Paint two more petals adjacent to it.

3. Using red buttercream in a piping bag, pipe small dots in the middle of the flower.

4. Paint two more broad, ruffled petals to finish off the flower

5. Using the small palette knife, pick up a very small amount of green buttercream and paint two or more small leaves to finish off the flower.

Icelandic poppy, painted

These poppies have nice, round petals that you can paint effortlessly using a rounded palette knife. You can play with a variety of buttercream colours to create entirely different looks here. Again, you will need a cocktail stick to create the leaf texture.

Buttercreams in pale pink and green; rounded and small palette knives; brown and yellow buttercreams in piping bags with holes cut at the top.

1

2
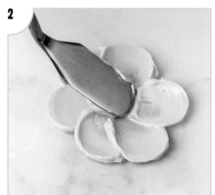

3

4

5

6

1. Using a rounded palette knife, pick up some buttercream on the back of the knife (see page 31). Place the palette knife flat on the surface and gently pull it inwards to paint a rounded petal.

2. Paint five or six overlapping petals in a circle.

3. Using brown buttercream in a piping bag, pipe some dots in a small circle around the centre of the flower.

4. Using a second piping bag, pipe yellow buttercream dots in the middle of the flower.

5. Using a small palette knife and some green buttercream, paint some leaves coming out from underneath the petals – see Tip, page 56.

6. Finally, add detailing to the leaves using a cocktail stick (toothpick).

Rose, painted

Roses are visually stunning when painted with palette knives. The play of two colours – a darker shade of buttercream for the inner petals and a lighter shade for the outer petals – is an important feature to keep in mind when it comes to painting roses.

Buttercreams in pale pink, dark pink and green; small palette knife.

1

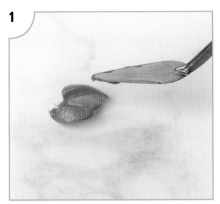

2

3

4

5

1. On a small palette knife, pick up some buttercream in a dark shade of pink (see page 31). Place the palette knife flat on the surface and gently move it in a curved formation. Paint two curved petals facing each other: this is the rosebud.

2. Paint curved petals all around the bud. Make sure that you work under the petals already painted so that you don't squash them. Paint three or four layers in the darker shade of buttercream.

3. Using the small palette knife, pick up some buttercream in a lighter shade of pink, and paint curved petals all around the rose.

4. Paint one or two more layers using the lighter shade of buttercream.

5. Finally, still using the small palette knife, pick up some green buttercream and paint two or more small leaves, in a similar way in which you might paint a narrow petal.

Tip
The more buttercream you use, the bigger and thicker your petals.

The Cakes

Autumn Cupcake
Collection, page 64

Christmas Cupcake
Wreath, page 72

Summer Basket,
page 80

Sunset Beauty,
page 86

Painted Wildflowers,
page 90

Summer Bouquet,
page 96

Birds and Blooms,
page 102

Hydrangea Lady,
page 108

Tropical Petal Cascade,
page 114

Majestic Beauty, page 120

Autumn Cupcake Collection

These cupcakes in yellow, orange and red shades feature sunflowers, heleniums, drop flowers, beautiful buttercream birds and autumnal leaves. It's like autumn on a plate!

YOU WILL NEED

- Cupcakes × 6
- Coloured buttercreams: yellow, light brown, dark brown, red, orange and green
- Palette knife
- Piping bags and couplers
- Cocktail sticks (toothpicks)
- Greaseproof paper
- Flower nail
- Wooden block (optional)
- Flower lifter
- Wilton 352 nozzle for leaves and sunflowers
- Wilton 3 for details
- Wilton 224 for drop flowers
- Wilton 104 for helenium

FLOWERS FEATURED

- Sunflowers × 2 (see page 36)
- Helenium 'Ruby Tuesday', (see pages 42–43)
- Drop flowers (see pages 34–35)

Sunflower cupcakes

You can pipe the flowers directly onto the cupcakes or pipe onto greaseproof paper on a flower nail, freeze them and then transfer them onto the cupcakes. Both options are given below, so you can choose which option works best for you.

Option 1: Transferring a flower onto a cupcake

When you are starting out, it is easier to pipe your flowers on a flower nail covered with greaseproof paper. Once you become comfortable with flower piping, however, you can try piping directly onto your cakes – see overleaf.

The directions for piping the sunflower, below, can be found on page 36.

1

2

3

4

1. Gently slide the greaseproof paper away from the flower nail.
2. Place the flower, still on the paper, on a plate or flat tray, then into the freezer for 15 minutes or so, until it is firm enough that you can pick it up and place it on your cake.
3. Once the flower is frozen, use a flower lifter to lift the flower gently from the greaseproof paper.
4. Carefully place the frozen flower on the cupcake. You can use a cocktail stick (toothpick) for support.

Option 2: Piping the flower directly onto the cupcake

1

2

3

1. You can also pipe the sunflower directly onto the cupcake – again, see page 36 for instructions on piping the petals.

2. Using dark brown buttercream with a Wilton 3 writing nozzle, fill the middle of the flower.

3. Finish off the flower by piping small dots – in light and dark brown buttercream – in the middle of the sunflower.

The second completed sunflower cupcake.

Helenium 'Ruby Tuesday' and drop flower cupcake

Follow the instructions on pages 42–43, and pages 34–35, to pipe a helenium and a drop flower, and place them on two further cupcakes.

The miniature wreath

1. Using a Wilton 3 writing nozzle, pipe strands of dark brown buttercream around the cupcake as the basis for a wreath.

2. Using orange buttercream and a Wilton 352 nozzle, pipe some simple autumnal leaves in groups of three around the wreath – see page 52.

3. Using green buttercream and a Wilton 352 nozzle, pipe green leaves around the wreath just behind each group of orange leaves.

4. Using red buttercream and a Wilton 224 nozzle, pipe a cluster of red drop flowers in the gaps between the leaves (see pages 34–35). Continue this all around the wreath.

5. Finally, using yellow buttercream and a Wilton 3 writing nozzle, pipe dots of yellow buttercream in the middle of the drop flowers.

The completed miniature wreath.

Wreath with birds

1. Similar to before (see page 67), pipe a wreath around the cupcake using brown buttercream. Using a piping bag with yellow buttercream and a Wilton 352 nozzle, pipe leaves around half of the cupcake.

2. Using a piping bag with green buttercream and a Wilton 352 nozzle, pipe green leaves in between the yellow leaves.

3. Using red buttercream and a Wilton 224 nozzle, pipe clusters of drop flowers in front of – and in between – the leaves, moving towards the centre of the cupcake.

4. Using a piping bag with yellow buttercream and a Wilton 3 writing nozzle, pipe dots of buttercream in the middle of each drop flower.

Piping the birds

You can pipe the bird on a flower nail paired with a greaseproof paper, freeze it and transfer it onto the cupcake or pipe the bird directly onto the cupcake. Both options are demonstrated below.

The birds and their features are piped from yellow and dark brown buttercream, using a Wilton 352 nozzle for the wings and a Wilton 3 writing nozzle for the eyes and beaks.

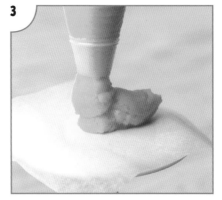

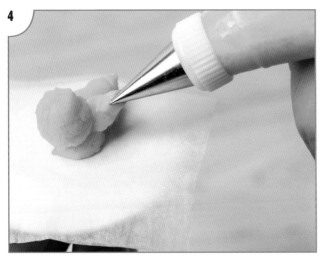

1. Using a piping bag filled with yellow buttercream (with no nozzle, just the coupler attachment), pipe a generous blob of buttercream onto a flower nail covered with a square of greaseproof paper.

2. Gently slide the piping bag out to the desired length of the bird's body.

3. Pipe a blob of buttercream on top for the bird's head.

4. Using yellow buttercream and a Wilton 352 nozzle, pipe a simple leaf-like structure for one wing of the bird, just where the head and body meet.

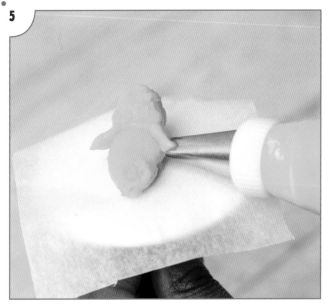

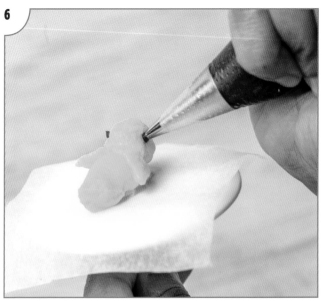

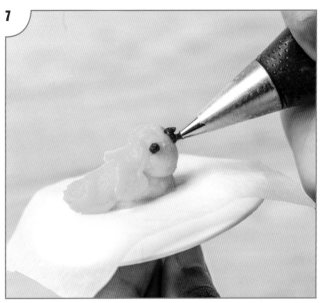

5. Pipe a similar wing on the other side of the bird's body.

6. Using brown buttercream and a Wilton 3 writing nozzle, pipe dots for eyes.

7. Pipe two small strands for a beak.

8. Finally, use a cocktail stick (toothpick) to smooth and shape the body. Put the bird in the freezer for 15 minutes or until it is firm to the touch, before transferring it to the cupcake.

The piped bird.

Adding the birds

1

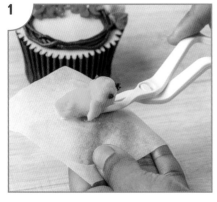

2

3

4

5

6

1. Use the flower lifter to gently lift the first bird off the greaseproof paper.

2. Carefully place the bird on the cupcake. Use a cocktail stick (toothpick) for support.

3. Pipe more leaves in yellow and green around the bird.

4. If you would prefer to pipe the second bird directly onto the cupcake, you can do so (following the steps on pages 69–70), starting with the body and the head.

5. Add the wings – like simple leaves – using a Wilton 352 nozzle.

6. Finally, using dark brown buttercream and a Wilton 3 writing nozzle, pipe dots for eyes and two tiny strands for a beak, as for the first bird. Your collection of cupcakes is now complete!

The completed wreath with birds.

Christmas Cupcake Wreath

This wreath makes a fabulous centrepiece for a Christmas dessert table. The pull-apart cupcake wreath features roses, poinsettias, pinecones, holly leaves, berries and baubles, all crafted in buttercream. Not only does this arrangement look gorgeous, you also don't have to worry about portion sizes or cutting cakes or any of that. Just pull the wreath apart and enjoy the delicious cupcakes.

YOU WILL NEED

❖ Cupcakes × 10

❖ Cake board

❖ Coloured buttercreams: green, red, ivory, yellow and brown (chocolate)

❖ Uncoloured buttercream

❖ Piping bags and couplers

❖ Greaseproof paper

❖ Flower nail

❖ Flower lifter

❖ Cocktail sticks (toothpicks)

❖ Wilton 352 nozzle for holly leaves, pinecones and poinsettia

❖ Wilton 233 for fir leaves

❖ Wilton 104 or 125 for roses

❖ Wilton 5 for berries

❖ Wilton 2 and 3 for details

FLOWERS FEATURED

❖ Roses, small × 2 and large × 2 (see pages 48–49)

❖ Poinsettias × 2 (see pages 38–39)

ADDITIONAL DETAILS

❖ Baubles × 2 (see page 76)

❖ Pinecones × 2 (see page 77)

Constructing the wreath

1

1. Arrange the cupcakes in a circle on a cake board. You can use as many cupcakes as you'd like depending on the size of the wreath. I have used 10 cupcakes here.

2. Using a Wilton 233 nozzle and green buttercream, pipe 1.5cm- ($^9/_{16}$in-) long strands of buttercream on the first cupcake to resemble fir leaves.

3. Start at one side of the cupcake, adding more layers over the leaves already piped.

4. Continue piping fir leaves until you have covered the cupcake completely.

5. Repeat the same process to cover all of the cupcakes in fir leaves.

The wreath, ready for embellishment.

Piping the holly leaves and berries

1. Using green buttercream and a Wilton 352 nozzle, pipe some holly leaves between the cupcakes, following the instructions on page 53.

2. Pipe holly leaves in sets of three between each pair of cupcakes.

3. Using red buttercream and a Wilton 5 nozzle, pipe three small blobs of buttercream resembling berries where the holly leaves meet.

4. Pipe berries all the way around the cupcake.

Making a bauble

Baubles can be created easily using buttercream: each bauble is simply a blob of buttercream, decorated with details. We will need two baubles for this cupcake wreath design.

1. Using a piping bag with a 1cm- (⅜in-) diameter hole cut at the end, pipe a blob of uncoloured buttercream onto a flower nail covered with greaseproof paper.

2. Using a piping bag with yellow buttercream and a Wilton 2 writing nozzle, pipe filigree-like details on the bauble.

3. Pipe filigree details all over the buttercream bauble. You can create any pattern of your choice. Repeat the steps to make a second bauble. Freeze the baubles until they are firm to the touch, before transferring them to the wreath.

Piping a pinecone

The pinecone is piped in brown (chocolate) buttercream, using the Wilton 352 nozzle.

The Wilton 352 nozzle.

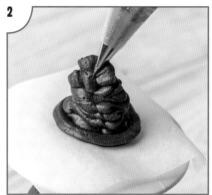

1. Using brown buttercream and the Wilton 352 nozzle, pipe a guide circle in the centre of a flower nail (covered with greaseproof paper).

2. Pipe a sturdy pyramid of buttercream over the guide circle.

3. Pipe simple leaf-like scales all around the pyramid structure, starting from the base.

4. Pipe more layers of scales to cover the whole pyramid.

5. Finish by piping a single upright scale at the tip of the pinecone. Repeat the steps to pipe a second pinecone for your wreath. Freeze the pinecones until they are firm to the touch, before transferring them to the wreath.

Adding the details onto the wreath

Pipe your flowers onto greaseproof paper and freeze them for 15 minutes or until they are firm to the touch. I have piped small red and large ivory roses – two of each – and two red poinsettia flowers.

To create a pleasing composition, you can place similar flowers opposite to each other in the circle. For example, the pinecones are placed opposite to each other, as are the pairs of roses, baubles and poinsettias.

1. Using a flower lifter, remove the roses from the greaseproof paper.

2. Place the roses, one by one, on the wreath. Use a cocktail stick (toothpick) for support.

3. Similarly, place the frozen baubles on the wreath.

4. Next to the baubles, you can place the pinecones.

5. Next, place the red poinsettias onto the wreath.

6. Repeat the same process to place any remaining flowers

7. Finally, pipe more leaves and berries (see page 75) to fill in any evident gaps between the flowers. Your Christmas cupcake wreath is complete.

Summer Basket

This is another pull-apart cupcake arrangement, with a twist. You can use the techniques in this project to create cupcake baskets of any shape and size. These baskets are perfect gifts – after all, what is more perfect than a collection of edible blooms?

Preparing the basket

1. Cut a wet foam block to the size of the basket using a knife, and cover it with plastic food wrap. This is to make the foam food-safe.

2. Cover the wet foam block with green tissue paper or paper napkins.

3. Place the covered wet foam block into the wicker basket and gently press it down into the basket.

4. Press cocktail sticks (toothpicks) into the foam block through the tissue – these will be used to hold the cupcakes in place.

Piping leaves and hydrangeas

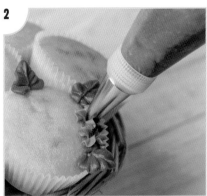

1. Using green buttercream and a Wilton 352 nozzle, pipe three simple leaves around the edge of the first cupcake, following the instructions on page 52.

2. Using purple buttercream and a Wilton 224 nozzle, pipe drop flowers onto the cupcake.

3. Cover the entire cupcake with drop flowers.

4. You can add more layers of drop flowers to add height and create a dome-like appearance.

5. Using yellow buttercream and a Wilton 3 nozzle, pipe dots into the middles of the individual drop flowers. Repeat these steps to add drop flowers and leaves to another three cupcakes.

Arranging the flowers on the cupcakes

There are no rules on how to place the flowers on the basket. I like to spread the colours evenly to create a visually pleasing effect.

1

2

3

4

5

6

1. Pipe your flowers onto greaseproof paper and freeze them for 15 minutes or until they are firm to the touch. Using a flower lifter, pick up the frozen flowers (here, a chrysanthemum) from the greaseproof paper.

2. Place the flowers on the cupcakes with leaves already piped (see page 82, step 1), sliding them off with a cocktail stick (toothpick) for support.

3. Continue to pipe leaves before you place any frozen flowers, so that the flowers are well supported.

4. Transfer your remaining, larger, frozen flowers to the cupcakes – such as begonias. Here, I am placing one of two pink begonias; you can pipe a third begonia in a different colour if you choose – such as yellow.

5. Place smaller flowers (such as the daisies) in between the cupcakes to fill any gaps.

6. Finally, pipe leaves in any gaps so that the flowers are well supported once they come to room temperature.

Piping and transferring a rose

Without freezing

Once you are comfortable piping flowers, you can pipe them onto a flower nail and transfer them directly onto a cake without having to freeze the flowers first.

Here, I am using the two-tone piping technique (see page 28) to pipe a rose in pink and yellow shades of buttercream. Note that you do not need to use greaseproof paper if you are transferring the flower directly from the flower nail to the cupcake.

1
2
3

1. Follow the instructions on pages 48–49 to pipe two large two-tone roses, using a Wilton 125 nozzle.

2. Using a flower lifter, gently lift each rose from the flower nail. Slide the rose off the flower nail onto the cupcake using a cocktail stick (toothpick).

3. Finally, pipe a couple of leaves underneath the rose to support and secure it further.

Completing the arrangement

Place your remaining piped flowers on the cupcakes. I have piped roses, begonias, chrysanthemums, daisies and drop flowers. Pipe leaves between the flowers to fill any evident gaps.

Placing the yellow begonia onto the cupcake.

Placing the second pink begonia onto the cupcake.

Filling any evident gaps with leaves.

Sunset Beauty

Piped buttercream peonies and cherry blossoms really pop on this abstract watercolour-effect cake. This one-tier beauty radiates elegance and can be created in a variety of colours to suit the mood of the occasion.

Covering the cake

A watercolour painting effect looks beautiful on a buttercream cake. It is easily achieved by layering different colours of buttercream on the cake. Here, we are covering the cake with pink buttercream.

YOU WILL NEED

❖ 20cm (8in) cake
❖ Coloured buttercreams: pink, light pink, red, pale yellow, dark green and light green
❖ Cake turntable
❖ Cake drum
❖ Palette knife – medium
❖ Cake smoother
❖ Piping bags and couplers
❖ Cocktail sticks (toothpicks)
❖ Flower nail
❖ Flower lifter
❖ Wilton 103 nozzle for cherry blossoms
❖ JEM 121 for peony
❖ Wilton 352 nozzle for leaves

FLOWERS FEATURED

❖ Cherry blossoms (see page 37)
❖ Peonies × 6 (see page 50)

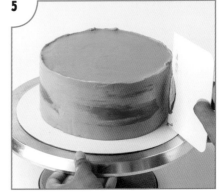

1. Layer a paler pink buttercream in patches over the side of the cake using a medium palette knife.

2. Use the same techniques to apply a layer of red buttercream in patches.

3. Hold a cake smoother vertically against the cake. Using the side of the smoother, lightly smooth the cake in sections while rotating the cake turntable.

4. Discard the excess buttercream in a bowl and carry on smoothing the cake in sections.

5. Make sure not to over-smooth and lose the definition of the different colours. You want them to merge ever so slightly but still show as individual colours.

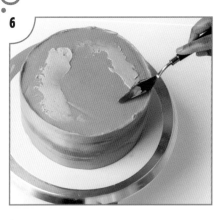

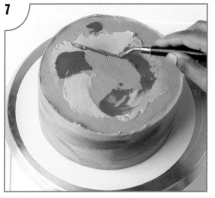

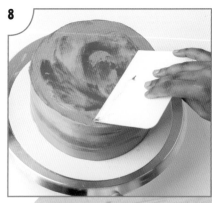

6. Use the same layering techniques on top of the cake, starting with light pink buttercream.

7. In a similar way, layer red buttercream on top of the cake.

8. Use a smoother to smooth the top of the cake. Make sure you keep the smoother flat on the cake and move it across the cake from one side to the other, with a very light touch.

The covered cake.

Adding the flowers

Pipe up to six peonies of varying sizes and in different shades of yellow and pink, following the instructions on page 50. Freeze the piped peonies on a tray for 15 minutes or so until they are firm enough to be picked up easily using a flower lifter.

Pipe several cherry blossoms, following the instructions on page 37, and freeze them until they are firm to the touch.

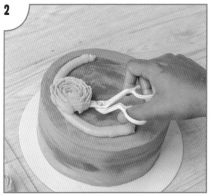

1. Pipe a crescent-shaped strand of light pink buttercream on the top of the cake. This is to give some height as well as to enable you to place the flowers at an angle.

2. Place the first, largest, peony on top and in the centre of the piped crescent.

3. Place a medium-sized peony on either side of the large peony. Use a cocktail (toothpick) to help you release the flowers onto the cake.

4. Place one of the smallest peonies onto the cake at the end of the crescent.

5. Arrange smaller peonies near the larger peonies, sliding them gently under any gaps between the piped crescent and the larger peonies. Filling gaps like this will ensure that when the bigger flowers come to room temperature they are supported and won't droop or collapse.

6. Place a few small peonies in front of the big flowers too.

7. Place frozen cherry blossoms on either side of the crescent of peonies.

Piping the last details

1. Using dark green buttercream and a Wilton 352 nozzle, pipe simple leaves in between the flowers (see page 52).

2. Next, pipe some light green coloured leaves. If there are gaps that you can see underneath the flowers, pipe a leaf there, so that when the flowers come to room temperature they don't collapse and are supported well by the leaves.

3. Using a two-tone piping bag (see page 28) and the Wilton 104 nozzle, pipe yellow-and-pink petals

4. Finally, using a Wilton 352 nozzle, pipe small pale-yellow petals around the base of the cake as a border.

Painted Wildflowers

This palette-knife painted cake features a clean, sleek design with a statement chrysanthemum in the middle paired with some cherry blossoms.

This design is perfect for one-tier cakes or even on bigger tiered cakes. You can really play with the colours too – there are no limits to how you can vary this design.

YOU WILL NEED

❖ 20cm (8in) cake

❖ Coloured buttercreams: blue, dark green, light green, orange, dark orange, yellow and red

❖ Uncoloured buttercream

❖ Cake drum

❖ Palette knives – small, medium and large

❖ Cake smoother

❖ Piping bags

❖ Coupler

❖ Wilton 3 writing nozzle for cake border

❖ Cocktail sticks (toothpicks)

FLOWERS FEATURED

❖ Chrysanthemums (see page 56)

❖ Cherry blossoms (see page 59)

Painting the leaves

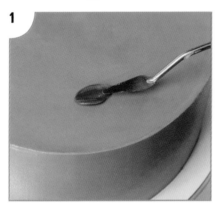

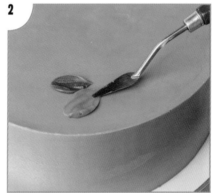

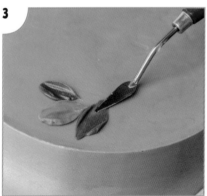

1. Pick up some dark green buttercream using a small palette knife (see page 31). Apply it gently, flat on the cake, to paint a leaf.

2. Paint a second leaf in light green buttercream, to contrast with the dark green.

3. Pipe a set of three leaves in alternating shades of green.

4. Repeat to form a crescent pattern around the top of the cake.

Painting the chrysanthemum

1. Using a large palette knife, pick up orange-coloured buttercream and start painting petals.

2. Apply the petals in a circular pattern next to each other. Make sure to apply them with even pressure, and avoid squashing or smudging the petals you've already painted.

3. Using a small palette knife, pick up dark orange-coloured buttercream, and paint smaller petals between each pair of larger petals.

4. Repeat in a circular pattern.

5. Using a piping bag with uncoloured buttercream and a hole cut at the end, pipe small dots in the middle of the flower.

Tip
Use a small, medium or large palette knife depending on the size of the flower you are painting,

Painting the cherry blossoms

1. Using a small palette knife, pick up some yellow buttercream and paint broader petals for cherry blossoms (see page 59).

2. Using a piping bag with red buttercream and a hole cut at the end, pipe small dots in the middle of the cherry blossom.

3. Paint two more yellow petals over the top and small green details at the bottom to finish off the blossom.

Adding leaves and leaf details

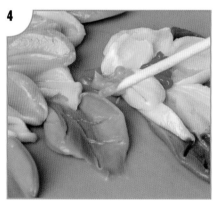

1. Pick up some dark and light green buttercream using a small palette knife and paint leaves coming from underneath the flowers to give a realistic look.

2. Repeat the same process for all the flowers, looking for gaps where you can naturally place the leaves. The trick is to be careful not to squash the petals.

3. Using a cocktail stick, draw lines to resemble the veins of the leaves.

4. Use the cocktail stick to smooth the stems of the flowers.

Adding buds and piping the cake border

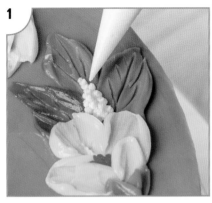

1. Using the piping bag containing the uncoloured buttercream (with a fine hole cut at the end), pipe small dots in between the flowers. These are filler elements that will bring the whole design together.

2. Using a piping bag with red buttercream and a Wilton 3 writing nozzle, pipe well-formed round dots all around the base of the cake as a border. This completes the project.

Summer Bouquet

This pretty pink cake features palette-knife painted roses and daisies, with piped lavender details. The chosen flowers represent love, purity and innocence; for the same reason, this design radiates a sense of calmness and serenity.

Painting the daisies

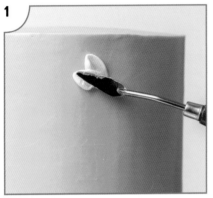

The daisies with piped centres.

1. Prepare, fill, crumb-coat and cover the 15cm (6in) double-barrel cake (see pages 16–20). Using a small palette knife and some white buttercream, begin to paint simple narrow petals to represent daisy petals (see page 57).

2. Paint more petals to form a circle.

3. Using a piping bag with some yellow buttercream and a hole cut at the end, pipe some dots in the middle of the flower.

YOU WILL NEED

❖ 15cm (6in) double-barrel cake
❖ Cake smoother
❖ Cake drum
❖ Coloured buttercreams: pink, dark pink, pale pink, white, yellow, green, light green and purple
❖ Piping bags
❖ Cocktail sticks (toothpicks)
❖ Palette knife – small

FLOWERS FEATURED

❖ Daisies (see page 57)
❖ Roses (see page 61)
❖ Lavender details (see page 100)

Painting the roses

1. Using a small palette knife, pick up some buttercream in the darkest shade of pink and paint curved petals facing each other. This is the rosebud (see page 61).

2. Continue painting curved petals all around the bud. Make sure that you work under the petals already painted so that you don't squash them.

3. Still using the small palette knife, pick up buttercream in a medium shade of pink and paint petals around the outside of the dark petals.

4. Paint one or two more layers using the lightest shade of pink buttercream.

5. Paint an angled view of a second rose, purely in the medium shade of pink buttercream, To paint the side view, simply paint some extra layers of petals at the bottom of the bloom.

Painting the leaves

1. Using the small palette knife, pick up some green buttercream. Now carefully place the palette knife underneath the painted rose petals, and in a single clean stroke, paint the leaves. See Tip, page 56.

2. You can paint two leaves facing each other to complete the roses.

3. Add more leaves in between the flowers by working underneath the painted petals.

The painted leaves.

Adding lavender details

1. Using a piping bag with a fine hole cut at the end, pipe tiny strands of purple buttercream facing each other, to give the effect of lavender.

2. You can use this technique to fill any obvious gaps in the design.

Adding the final details

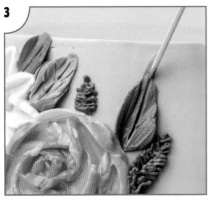

1. Using a small palette knife, pick up a lighter shade of green buttercream. Carefully place the palette knife next to the painted dark green leaves to paint in some lighter leaves.

2. Repeat the process across the design. The two shades of green leaves will add more character.

3. Using a cocktail stick (toothpick), add more details on the leaves, such as veins.

4. Finally, use the cocktail stick (toothpick) to etch in some fronds, to give more texture to the design.

Birds and Blooms

This is a fun cake that combines both the palette-knife painting and piping techniques. The piped cherry blossoms against a sky-blue cake and the birds perching on the branches truly radiate spring vibes.

YOU WILL NEED

❖ 15cm (6in) double-barrel cake for bottom tier

❖ 10cm (4in) cake for top tier

❖ Dowels × 4 (see page 21)

❖ Cake smoother

❖ Cake drum

❖ Cake turntable

❖ Coloured buttercreams: blue, white, brown (chocolate), yellow, purple, pink, red and dark green

❖ Paper tissue

❖ Piping bags and couplers

❖ Cocktail sticks (toothpicks)

❖ Palette knife for cake decorating

❖ Palette knives for painting – small

❖ Wilton 5 nozzle for details

❖ Wilton 103 for cherry blossoms

❖ Wilton 352 for the leaves

FLOWERS FEATURED

❖ Cherry blossoms (see page 37)

Covering the cake

1

2

3

4

1. Prepare, fill, crumb-coat and cover the 15cm (6in) double-barrel cake (see pages 16–20). For a two-tone cake covering, layer the buttercreams as shown: using a piping bag with a 1cm- (⅜in-) diameter hole cut at the end, pipe four strands of blue buttercream around the base of the bottom tier of the cake.

2. Using a piping bag with a 1cm- (⅜in-) diameter hole cut at the end, pipe two strands of white buttercream above the blue strand.

3. Cover the sides of the cake, alternating the blue and white buttercreams.

4. Repeat the process on the top of the cake.

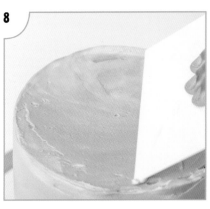

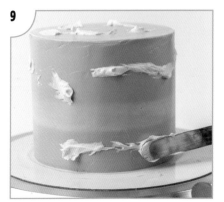

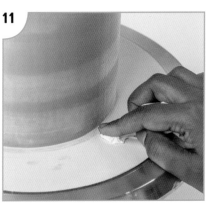

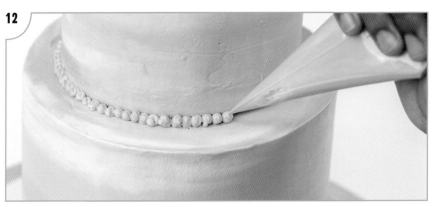

5. Using a palette knife, loosely smooth the buttercream on the top of the cake.

6. Similarly, smooth the buttercream around the side of the cake.

7. Place a cake smoother against the cake and slowly smooth one section at a time, while rotating the turntable. Repeat until the whole side of the cake is smooth.

8. Smooth the buttercream on the top of the cake, using the smoother.

9. Using the palette knife, apply some more white buttercream in patches over the blue buttercream areas, for clouds.

10. Smooth the white areas. Be careful not to oversmooth and lose the definition of the individual colours. Repeat steps 1–10 on the smaller, top tier of the cake.

11. Use a paper tissue to clean the cake drum.

12. Stack the two tiers of the cake using the four dowels (see page 21). Using a piping bag with a fine hole cut at the end, and blue buttercream, pipe beads all round where the tiers meet.

Piping the branches

1. Using a Wilton 5 nozzle and brown (chocolate) buttercream, pipe strands of buttercream to resemble the trunk of a cherry blossom tree.

2. Pipe the strands all the way up to the top of the cake.

3. Pipe a few additional strands on top of the trunk for added texture.

4. Pipe a branch leading off to one side, where one of your birds will sit.

Sketching and piping the birds

It is very easy to sketch the birds freehand, but if you are less confident in doing this, you can draw a template first and scribe around it, as with the *Hydrangea Lady* on page 108.

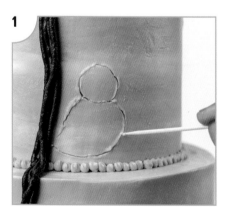

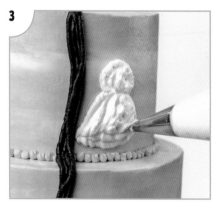

1. To sketch the first bird directly onto the cake, at the base of the top tier, all you need to do is draw a circle for the head and a slanted heart shape for the body.

2. Using a Wilton 5 nozzle and some white buttercream, fill in the head and body of the bird.

3. Pipe some more buttercream over the middle of the body and the head to give more height, and a domed appearance.

4

5

6

7

8

4. Using a small palette knife, gently smooth the buttercream.

5. Using a piping bag with a fine hole cut at the end, and yellow buttercream, add some details on the top of the head, and suggest the wings of the bird.

6. Using a small palette knife, gently smooth the yellow buttercream, then add a feather-like texture.

7. Add some purple details to the bottom of the bird's body using a small palette knife.

8. Using a piping bag with a fine hole cut at the end, and brown buttercream, pipe dots for eyes and small strands for a beak. Repeat steps 1–8 to sketch and pipe a second bird sitting on the branch.

The piped birds.

Piping the cherry blossoms and adding final touches

1

2

3

4

5

6

7

8
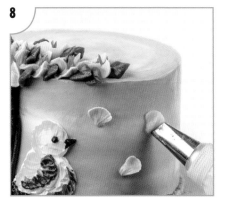

Note

For the cherry blossoms, I am again alternating between a pair of two-tone piping bags: one containing pink and white buttercreams, the other containing yellow and white. See page 28 for guidance on filling the two-tone piping bags.

1. Using a two-tone piping bag with a Wilton 103 nozzle, pipe five-petal cherry blossom flowers on the top tier of the cake, in the pink and white buttercreams first. (See page 37.)

2. Pipe some more cherry blossoms, this time in the yellow and white buttercreams. Alternate between the two two-tone piping bags so that you start to see a good mix of colours.

3. Using a piping bag with a fine hole cut at the end, and red buttercream, pipe dots in the centres of the flowers.

4. Using dark green buttercream and a Wilton 352 nozzle, pipe simple leaves underneath the flowers (see page 52).

5. Pipe more cherry blossoms onto the tiers and the branches beneath the birds.

6. Pipe simple leaves into any visible gaps.

7. Use some purple buttercream to add some details on the wings.

8. Using both two-tone piping bags with a Wilton 103 nozzle attached to each, pipe simple fan-shaped individual petals in alternating colours, all over the cake, as falling petals. This completes the project.

Hydrangea Lady

This design combines palette-knife painting and piping techniques to create a dramatic floral cake, all in buttercream. You can alter the colours of the dress according to the occasion – a white gown would be perfect for a wedding cake.

I have used peach colour buttercream, achieved by adding a very small amount of pink gel colour to the buttercream. The natural yellow of buttercream plus a little pink creates the peach colour.

I have created this cake by stacking a 10cm (4in) cake over a 15cm (6in) dowelled double-barrel cake. Refer to page 21 to see how to stack a cake using dowels.

YOU WILL NEED

* 15cm (6in) double-barrel cake for bottom tier
* 10cm (4in) cake for top tier
* Cake smoother
* Cake drum
* Dowels × 4 (see page 21)
* Coloured buttercreams: peach, ivory, dark ivory, dark pink, light pink, brown (chocolate), white, purple, yellow, green and dark green
* Piping bags and couplers
* Cocktail sticks (toothpicks)
* Greaseproof paper
* Palette knife – small
* Paintbrush
* Flower lifter
* Wilton 103 nozzle for hydrangeas
* Wilton 3 writing nozzle for the lady's hair
* Wilton 352 nozzle for the leaves

FLOWERS FEATURED

* Hydrangeas (see pages 40–41)

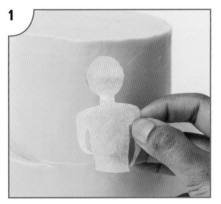
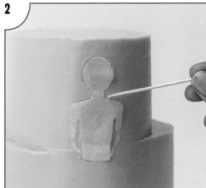
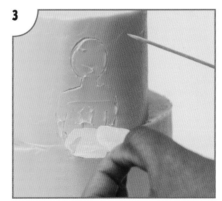

1. Prepare, fill, crumb-coat and cover the two tiers of the cake with peach buttercream (see pages 16–20). Stack them following the instructions on page 21. Trace the template of the lady's upper body, right, onto greaseproof paper.

2. Hold the template against the top tier of the cake and use a cocktail stick (toothpick) to scribe the outline onto the cake.

3. Gently take the template off the cake. If the cake is frozen, the template will come away easily; if not, the buttercream will be softer, so some may come away with the greaseproof paper. Don't worry if this happens, however, as you will be painting over the scribed design.

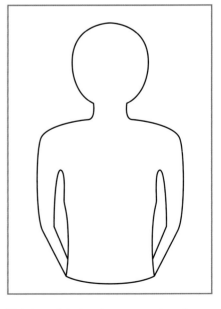

This template has been reproduced at full size.

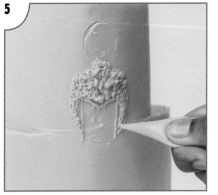

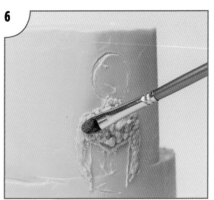

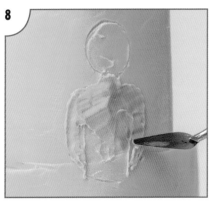

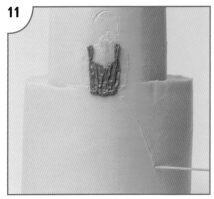

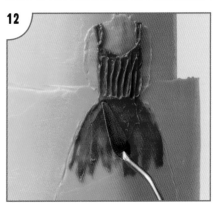

4. Using a piping bag with a fine hole cut at the end, and ivory buttercream, pipe around the outline of the traced shape of the lady's upper body.

5. Fill the shape with ivory buttercream.

6. Using a paintbrush, lightly smooth the buttercream.

7. Using a darker shade of ivory buttercream in a piping bag, add some shadow details to the body.

8. Use a small palette knife to lightly smooth this.

9. Using a piping bag with a fine hole cut at the end and dark pink buttercream, pipe and fill the bodice of the dress. Pipe two straps, one over each shoulder.

10. Use a palette knife to smooth the bodice lightly and add texture to the dress.

11. Use a cocktail stick (toothpick) to scribe a rough outline over the bottom tier of the cake, for the skirt of the dress.

12. In a similar manner to the bodice, fill the very top of the skirt with dark pink buttercream and smooth it using the small palette knife.

13

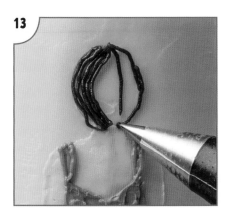

14

13. Using a piping bag with a Wilton 3 nozzle, pipe tiny strands of brown (chocolate) buttercream onto the lady's head for hair.

14. Pipe overlapping strands to create texture.

15. Next, pipe strands of buttercream in a circle, to resemble a hairdo such as a low bun.

16. Finally, pipe three dots in dark pink buttercream on top of the bun to suggest flowers in the lady's hair.

15

16

Creating the hydrangea gown

Note that I am alternating between two two-tone piping bags to create the hydrangeas – one of dark pink and white buttercream, and another of purple and dark pink buttercream. See page 28 for details on filling the piping bags, and pages 40–41 for instructions on piping the hydrangea blossoms.

1

2

1. Using a two-tone piping bag (see page 28) with a Wilton 103 nozzle, pipe four-petal hydrandea blossoms over the skirt, beginning just above where the dark pink buttercream area ends.

2. Alternate between the two piping bags so that you get a mix of both colours of flowers.

3

4

5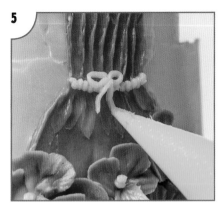

6

3. Fill any gaps with single petals.

4. Using a piping bag with a fine hole cut at the end, and yellow buttercream, pipe dots in the middles of the flowers

5. Using a piping bag with a fine hole cut at the end, and yellow buttercream, pipe a waistband and a bow onto the gown.

6. Finally, using a piping bag with a fine hole cut at the end, and light pink buttercream, pipe tiny dots to create sleeves on the gown.

Completing the cake

1

2

3

1. Pipe and freeze a globe of four-petal hydrangeas in two-tone (purple and pink) buttercream (see pages 40–41). Using a flower lifter, gently transfer it onto the top of the cake.

2. Using a piping bag with dark green buttercream and a Wilton 352 nozzle, pipe simple leaves (see page 52).

3. Pipe more four-petal hydrangea flowers in between the leaves to create a seamless look. Do this on both the top of the cake, and over the skirt of the gown.

4

5

6

4. Using the piping bag with a fine hole cut at the end, and yellow buttercream, pipe dots in the middle of these additional flowers.

5. Using dark green buttercream and a Wilton 352 nozzle, pipe simple leaves underneath the flowers at the bottom of the gown.

6. Using the two two-tone piping bags with Wilton 103 nozzles, pipe simple fan-shaped petals all over the cake, like falling petals. Again, alternate between two piping bags: one filled with dark pink and white buttercreams, another filled with purple and dark pink buttercreams. This completes the cake.

The completed hydrangeas on the cake.

Tropical Petal Cascade

This colourful cake features free-flowing piped gladioli and palette-knife painted asters down the length of the cake. This design is extremely easy to do, not at all time-consuming, yet the results are quite striking.

The three big gladioli create structure for this design. The rest of the petals and the painted asters go around them. Be mindful of the distribution of colours, for example – the purple asters should be spread out evenly throughout the pattern.

YOU WILL NEED

❖ 20cm (8in) cake for bottom tier
❖ 10cm (4in) double-barrel cake for top tier
❖ Cake smoother
❖ Cake drum
❖ Coloured buttercreams: dark green, red, brown (chocolate), yellow, dark pink, light pink and purple
❖ Piping bags and couplers
❖ Cocktail sticks (toothpicks)
❖ Palette knives – small
❖ Wilton 102 nozzle for leaves
❖ Wilton 104 for gladioli

FLOWERS FEATURED

❖ Gladiolus (see page 45)
❖ Asters (see page 58)

Piping the leaves

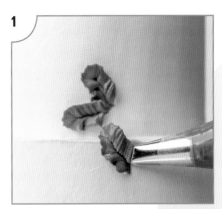

1. Using a Wilton 102 nozzle and dark green buttercream, pipe pairs of ruffled leaves over the front of the cake (see page 54).

2. Using a cocktail stick (toothpick), sketch circles to indicate where you'd like to pipe the flowers.

Piping the gladioli

1

2

3

4

5

6

1. Using a piping bag with a Wilton 104 nozzle and red buttercream, pipe the first gladiolus flower at the top of the upper tier.

2. Using a piping bag with a fine hole cut at the end, and yellow buttercream, pipe small dots into the middle of the flower.

3. Using a piping bag with a fine hole cut at the end, and brown buttercream, pipe small dots into the centre to add more detail.

4. Using a Wilton 104 nozzle and a two-tone piping bag of dark pink and light pink buttercreams, pipe a second gladiolus flower beneath the first.

5. Add detailing to the middle of the flower in yellow and brown buttercreams, as in steps 2 and 3.

6. Next to the first two gladiolus flowers, pipe single as well as pairs of ruffled leaf-like petals along the length of the cake, using the Wilton 104 nozzle. See page 54 for guidance on piping the ruffled petals.

Painting the asters

1. Using a small palette knife and purple buttercream, paint asters in between the gladioli and leaves, following the instructions on page 58.

2. Paint some full flowers and some half-flowers down the full length of the cake.

3. Using a piping bag with a fine hole cut at the end, and yellow buttercream, pipe small dots in the centres of the asters.

Piping the stems

1. Using a piping bag with a fine hole cut at the end, pipe small strands of brown (chocolate) buttercream, connecting the smaller flowers to the bigger ones. This is to unify the cake design and to add some extra texture.

2. Repeat the process all the way down the cake.

This technique can be used to fill any gaps in between the flowers, too.

Piping additional leaves

1. Using a Wilton 103 nozzle and dark green buttercream, pipe ruffled leaves next to any single as well as paired gladioli petals (see page 54).

2. Make sure to go underneath the piped flower petals to pipe the leaves.

3. Finally, pipe similar, small, leaves next to the asters. This completes the project.

Majestic Beauty

True to its name, this final design is quite grandiose. The deep purple tone creates a regal backdrop for the colourful florals, both palette-knife painted and piped. This design features free-flowing flowers – Icelandic poppies and chrysanthemums – and fantasy floral petals to give the cake an abstract twist.

Piping the leaves

1. Using a Wilton 102 nozzle and dark green buttercream, pipe simple leaves down the front of the cake (see page 54).

2. Pipe leaves in groups of three all the way down the front of the cake.

YOU WILL NEED

❖ 20cm (8in) double-barrel cake for bottom tier

❖ 15cm (6in) double-barrel cake for middle tier

❖ 10cm (4in) cake for top tier

❖ Cake smoother

❖ Cake drum

❖ Coloured buttercreams: purple, dark green, pink, brown (chocolate), yellow and red

❖ Uncoloured buttercream

❖ Piping bags and couplers

❖ Cocktail sticks (toothpicks)

❖ Rounded palette knives

❖ Wilton 102 and 352 nozzles for the leaves

❖ Wilton 104 and 103 nozzles for the free-flowing petals

❖ Wilton 81 for chrysanthemums

FLOWERS FEATURED

❖ Icelandic poppies (see page 60)

❖ Chrysanthemums × 7 (see pages 46–47)

❖ Cherry blossoms (see page 37)

Painting the Icelandic poppies

1

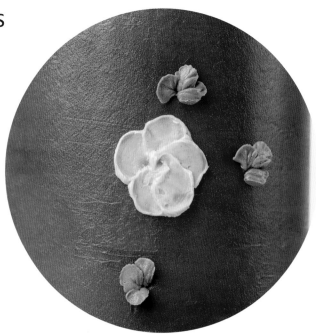

The first Icelandic poppy, painted.

2

3

1. In between the piped leaves, paint a few five-petal Icelandic poppies in pink (see page 60).

2. Using a piping bag with a fine hole cut at the end, and brown buttercream, pipe small dots in a circle to define the middle of the flower.

3. Using a piping bag with a fine hole cut at the end, and yellow buttercream, pipe small dots inside the ring of brown buttercream.

Piping the red blossoms

These are not specific flowers, but single and pairs of wavy petals.

1. Use the Wilton 104 nozzle and red buttercream to pipe on the red blossoms to give a free-flowing floral cascade effect

2. Using a piping bag with a fine hole cut at the end, pipe two strands of yellow buttercream coming from the lower tip of the red petals.

3. Repeat, all the way down the cake

Placing the first chrysanthemums

Pipe and freeze six chrysanthemums until firm to the touch, following the instructions on pages 46–47.

1. Using a piping bag with a 1cm- (³/₈in-) hole cut at the end, pipe a blob of uncoloured buttercream where the tiers meet. This is to give added height so that you can place the blooms in an angle.

2. Transfer the first chryanthemum onto the cake using a flower lifter.

3. Use a cocktail stick (toothpick) for support while you transfer each flower onto the cake.

Piping more leaves

1

2

3

1. Using a Wilton 352 nozzle and dark green buttercream, pipe simple leaves underneath the transferred chrysanthemums (see page 52).

2. Pipe a leaf into any gaps you can see under the flowers to ensure that the flowers will be supported once they come to room temperature.

3. Carry on piping leaves underneath all of the chrysanthemums.

Building up the composition

1

2

3

1. Using a piping bag with a 1cm- (³/₈in-) hole cut at the end, pipe a blob of uncoloured buttercream on top of the cake.

2. Transfer two more piped, frozen chrysanthemums onto the blob of buttercream, using a flower lifter and cocktail stick (toothpick).

3. Using a Wilton 352 nozzle and dark green buttercream, pipe simple leaves underneath the transferred chrysanthemums (see page 52).

Piping a chrysanthemum onto the cake

You can pipe a chrysanthemum directly onto the cake as well; however, I would recommend you do this this only after you are comfortable piping them. Freezing and transferring the flowers is the easier option.

1

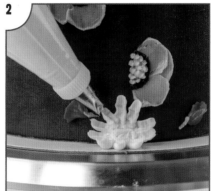
2

3

4

1. Using Wilton 81 nozzle and some uncoloured buttercream, pipe and fill a guide circle.

2. Pipe pulled petals all around the circle.

3. Pipe more layers of petals to complete the chrysanthemum (see pages 46–47).

4. Finish off by piping leaves underneath the flower.

Piping floating petals

Using a Wilton 103 nozzle and uncoloured buttercream, pipe single as well as pairs of petals all the way down the cake. This is to add a free-flowing petal effect. Follow the instructions for piping cherry blossom petals on page 37.

Adding stems

1. Using a piping bag with a fine hole cut at the end, pipe small strands of yellow buttercream connecting the floating petals to the main flowers.

2. Repeat this for all the petals on the cake. This will both unify the design and add some extra texture.

Painting two-tone leaves

To paint two-tone leaves, all you have to do is pick up a little of each of the two colours on the back of the palette knife and smooth the buttercream before painting (as shown on page 31).

1. Using a small palette knife, pick up some green and yellow buttercream (see page 31).

2. Paint simple narrow leaves all the way down the cake, making sure you go underneath the painted Icelandic poppies (see Tip, page 56).

Adding the final details

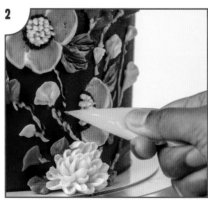

1. Using a cocktail stick (toothpick), add some vein-like textures to the leaves.

2. Using a piping bag with a fine hole cut at the end, pipe small strands of yellow buttercream to fill any gaps in the design. This completes the cake.

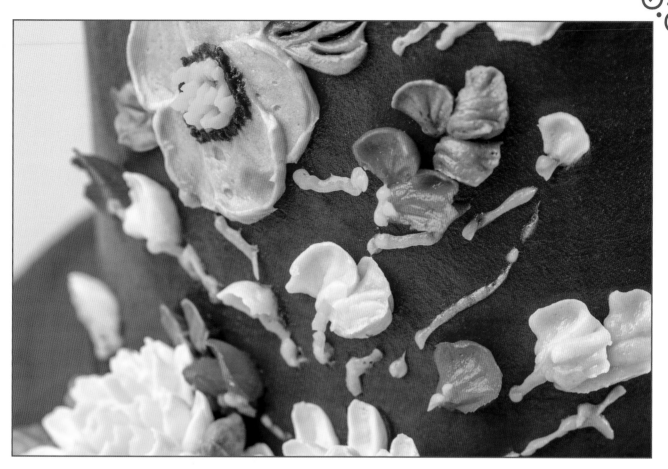

Index